# WEIGHT TRAINING

# BY DESIGN

# WEIGHT TRAINING

# BY DESIGN

## Create Your Own Individualized
## Workout Plan Using the
## Revolutionary BAM Superset™ System

## DALE GREENWALD, CSCS & ERIK MILLER, CPT

*McGraw·Hill*

New York   Chicago   San Francisco   Lisbon   London   Madrid   Mexico City
Milan   New Delhi   San Juan   Seoul   Singapore   Sydney   Toronto

The **McGraw·Hill** Companies

**Library of Congress Cataloging-in-Publication Data**

Greenwald, Dale.
   Weight training by design : customize your own fitness and weight loss program using the revolutionary BAM superset™ method / Dale Greenwald & Erik Miller.
      p.   cm.
   Includes index.
   ISBN 0-07-145888-3
   1. Weight training.   I. Miller, Erik.   II. Title.

   GV546.G74    2006
   613.7'13—dc22                                    2005007272

1 2 3 4 5 6 7 8 9 0   DOC/DOC   0 9 8 7 6 5

ISBN 0-07-145888-3

Photographs by Melissa Collins and Erik Miller.

McGraw-Hill books are available at special quantity discounts to use as premiums and sales promotions, or for use in corporate training programs. For more information, please write to the Director of Special Sales, Professional Publishing, McGraw-Hill, Two Penn Plaza, New York, NY 10121-2298. Or contact your local bookstore.

Medical Warning
Consult your physician or health care professional before beginning this, or any, exercise program. Not all exercise programs are suitable for everyone. Discontinue any exercise that causes you discomfort or pain and consult a medical expert. The instructions and advice presented in this book are in no way a substitute for medical counseling. The creators, writers, and distributors of this book disclaim any liabilities in connection with the exercises and advice herein.

BAM Superset System® is registered to Dale Greenwald.
Cybex® is registered to Cybex International, Inc.
Hammer Strength® is registered to Brunswick Corp.
Butt Blaster® is registered to Leg Tech, Inc.
Daily Dozen™ is a trademark of Dale Greenwald.

This book is printed on acid-free paper.

# contents

# Contents

# foreword

Numerous books and handbooks have been written regarding strength training and conditioning. But there are few that combine sound scientific principles and simple instructions in a very easy-to-read and practical format as *Weight Training by Design* does. Dale Greenwald and Erik Miller have combined their expertise to provide a guide on how to design and perform workouts in a safe and effective manner. The authors are knowledgeable and accurate in their anatomy, biomechanics, and applied physiology directed at fundamental principles in strength and conditioning.

Through the years I have taken care of many elite athletes as well as recreational athletes. They typically see me once they have had an injury. Consistently, they tend to share that they are looking for guidance on how to prevent injuries. I have not come across a more pertinent book than this to respond to that need. The discussion of proper techniques in training throughout the book is extremely helpful. I particularly like Chapter 2, "The Chapter of Lists," which provides a very good explanation of what to avoid when setting out on a training program.

The BAM Superset is a new concept to most athletes and makes good common sense. By combining various opposing muscle groups, the body gets an excellent workout without early fatigue. This is important for anyone who sets out to do an efficient weight training and conditioning program. It also applies to the majority of sporting activities since not one single muscle group is isolated, but in reality a combination of muscle groups are utilized for active movements.

Easy to understand, *Weight Training by Design* is quite applicable to all: from the novice in the weight room to the master athlete who has extensive experience in lifting and training; from the executive with only a few hours a week to work out to the athlete who lives and breathes working out; and from the high school athlete to the professional athlete.

I believe this book will become a well-used reference in all fitness and weight room facilities. I wholeheartedly recommend it and look forward to incorporating these principles in the training of the athletes I take care of, as well as in my own personal workouts. I tip my hat to these authors for their contributions in advancing the science and communication of strength training through this book.

—Eric McCarty, M.D.
  Chief, Sports Medicine and Shoulder Surgery, and Associate Professor, University of Colorado School of Medicine; Head Team Physician, University of Colorado and University of Denver

# acknowledgments
# and special thanks

Our families and clients.

Our great exercise models:
   Charlie George
   Darin Olien
   Kristy Wahlberg

Photographers:
   Melissa Collins (melissa-photo@hotmail.com)
   Erik Miller

Facility where photos were taken:
   Mountain's Edge Fitness in Boulder, Colorado

Special thanks to:
   Better Posture (www.betterposture.com) for use of their materials in Chapter 3.

# introduction

During the past 20 years of observing and instructing people in gyms and health clubs, we have seen the ways in which individuals go about their workouts. We have seen people who measure their success by the amount of weight they can lift, often sacrificing proper form, which can reduce the effective targeting of muscles and can be unsafe. We have met people who, because of an injury, shy away from a weight training program. We have also encountered people who have given up on their workouts because they became discouraged by their inability to obtain the goals that they desire. Many of these people were not sure how to properly design and implement their workouts.

The goal of this book is to provide a "road map" for you to effectively design and perform your own individualized workout, one that will enable you to attain the goals you desire and to see real results. In addition, this book can be an extremely useful tool for those who are recovering from injuries and may be reluctant to continue with or to start a resistive training program.

Regardless of the best intentions, you are bound to encounter several hurdles in your attempt to achieve your desired fitness goals. Obstacles typically encountered include time schedules, muscle soreness, and injuries. By implementing an appropriate workout design, you can overcome these obstacles. The key element in our design is what we call the Balanced Antagonistic Muscle (BAM) Superset. This is not the traditional superset.

The standard definition of a *superset* is the combination of two to three different exercises to be performed consecutively. These supersets are often composed of similar exercises, working and fatiguing the same group of muscles. The BAM Superset model we utilize is superior to this standard superset in that our technique highlights combining opposing muscle group exercises. Examples of

BAM Supersets include supersetting the biceps with the triceps or supersetting the quadriceps with the hamstrings.

There are many benefits to the BAM Superset approach. The foremost of these is the efficient use of time. Utilizing the BAM Superset technique eliminates the need for prolonged rest between sets. After performing a given exercise in the superset, the muscle tissue just being trained recovers while the opposing muscles are worked in a complementary exercise. This technique also produces a more balanced muscle fatigue across a given joint, helping to reduce muscle soreness. In addition, the balanced muscular development that is achieved will help to reduce the likelihood of injury.

Regardless of time constraints, skill level, or desired goals, the BAM Superset technique can be utilized in a wide variety of workouts. It allows for flexibility and variation in any workout design. Examples of BAM Superset exercise combinations are provided in Chapter 11, "Designing Your Own Workout." The specific weekly workout designs presented in that chapter provide several BAM Superset options.

From our perspective, the largest hurdle in a successful resistive training program is a general lack of understanding and knowledge. Improper technique and the inability to isolate specific muscle groups are the most common shortcomings. Because of this, the majority of this book emphasizes proper techniques for a wide range of machine* and free-weight exercises. These exercises cover all of the major body parts and will help you to design a complete workout regimen. We have selected the exercises that we feel are best suited to provide both a biomechanically correct and effectively sound workout without sacrificing safety or putting any undue stresses on the body.

# Introduction

We are confident that the flexibility and variation in workout design associated with the BAM Superset technique will allow you to design a workout that works for you. That personalized workout, coupled with the additional information on nutrition, posture, and lifestyle provided in this book, will enable you to achieve the goals you desire.

*We have selected Cybex equipment for the majority of the machine exercises in this book. We feel that Cybex is the most efficient equipment on the market due to its superior biomechanical design. However, if you do not have access to Cybex equipment, the techniques presented in this book can be applied to other brands of exercise equipment.

# WEIGHT TRAINING

# BY DESIGN

# chapter one

# 3 keys to a successful exercise program

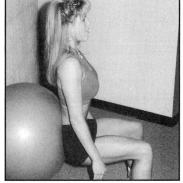

THINGS YOU WILL LEARN IN THIS CHAPTER:

**CARDIOVASCULAR TRAINING**

**DIET: NO NONSENSE INFORMATION**

**3-DAY SAMPLE EATING SCHEDULE**

**IMPORTANCE OF REST**

# 3 keys to a successful exercise program

Three components are necessary in order to achieve success in any exercise program: resistive training, cardiovascular training (cardio), and a healthy diet. To enhance these three components, adequate rest is necessary.

As a starting point, this chapter highlights cardio, diet, and rest. Resistive training is emphasized throughout the rest of the book.

## CARDIOVASCULAR TRAINING

Cardiovascular exercise (exercise involving the heart, vascular system, and lungs) is essential to any fitness program and to maintaining a healthy lifestyle. Two key factors to consider are (1) frequency and duration and (2) variations in intensity and the type of exercise selected.

### FREQUENCY AND DURATION

We recommend doing some form of cardio daily. The duration should vary with a minimum of 30 minutes in any one session. However, if you are just beginning an exercise program or have any health or physical limitations, the frequency is the most important factor. It is best to do some form of cardio exercise daily, building up the duration and intensity levels gradually as individual limitations allow.

### VARIATIONS IN INTENSITY AND EXERCISE SELECTION

When performing your daily cardio, we recommend implementing a variation in intensity level coupled with a variation in exercise selection. Cardio or aerobic intensity is typically gauged with respect to heart rate, specifically gauged with respect to the percentage of maximum heart rate.

Maximum heart rate varies from individual to individual and significantly between males and females of the same age. Because of this, we will not present any of the available general formulas for maximum heart rate as they do not handle this variability well. Maximum heart rate can be determined by testing under professionally supervised conditions. One method is to determine your lactate threshold and extrapolate from there. This is accomplished by drawing and analyzing blood during a graded exercise test.

Intense cardio training (where the heart rate can go above 85 percent maximum heart rate), such as high-intensity interval training, spinning, intense running, hard elliptical machine work, and high-impact aerobics, should be performed no more than two to three times a week.

During these intense cardio workouts, the body can cross the anaerobic threshold, or lactate threshold. At this point, the body can no longer metabolize blood lactate fast enough and that blood lactate level rises suddenly. This buildup is detrimental to muscle tissue, function, and recovery. If recovery time is not sufficient, training results will be counterproductive ("overtraining").

The remaining cardio days (four to five days a week) should be at a lower intensity, staying below or well below the anaerobic threshold (generally below 80 percent maximum heart rate). These days might include brisk walking, jogging (treadmill or outdoor), hiking, or biking (stationary bike or outdoor).

To achieve the maximum benefit, it is important to accurately monitor your heart rate throughout your workout. We highly recommend using a digital heart rate monitor, such as those made by Polar. Digital heart rate monitors help to eliminate the guesswork, or uncertainty, that can occur when you attempt to determine your heart rate by taking your own pulse.

## COMBING CARDIO WITH RESISTANCE TRAINING

A frequently asked question is whether one should do cardio exercise or resistance training (weight lifting) first. In general, if cardio is done first, strength levels will be reduced by an average of 15 percent. However, if you have injuries or find it difficult to warm up your body prior to lifting, starting with cardio might be a wise choice. We advise against doing intense cardio sessions on the days that you lift, as there is not enough energy stored in your body to do both.

If you choose to lift first, it is important to warm up your body by doing five to ten minutes of cardio first. Warming up not only helps prevent injuries, it helps your muscles work more efficiently—similar to warming up your car on a cold day.

# DIET: NO-NONSENSE INFORMATION

It should be noted that we are not registered dietitians, nor do we claim to be. However, we would like to present a useful, straightforward approach to healthy eating to enhance your exercise program. If you need more information on diet, we recommend you consult a registered dietitian.

## HYDRATION

One of the most important things you can do for your body is stay hydrated. The best source of hydration is water, not soft drinks and not juices. On average, an adult should drink 64 to 100 ounces of water per day. Maintaining hydration levels during exercise is especially important as it helps to prevent cramping and headaches and it helps to sustain your energy level.

## PROTEINS

In resistance training, the muscle tissue is actually being broken down during the workout. Following the workout, the muscle tissue needs to undergo recovery and growth. Proteins contain amino acids, which are the building blocks required for this recovery and growth. The timing of the protein intake following an exercise routine is critical. You should ingest protein within 30 to 60 minutes of completing a workout. The best sources of protein are organic meats, fish, and poultry, as well as that found in isolate whey protein supplements. If you are a vegetarian, whey protein supplements are a good alternative.

## GOOD FAT/BAD FAT

Essential fatty acids (EFAs), namely Omega acids 3 and 6, are just that—essential to your body's function. The absence of these EFAs in your diet will have an adverse affect on muscle function. Excellent sources of EFAs are cold-water fish and free-range beef and game. Cod liver oil and flaxseed oil supplements are also good sources of EFAs.

Partially hydrogenated oils (trans-fatty acids) and processed saturated fats are detrimental to body function and performance and should be avoided.

## GOOD CARBS/BAD CARBS

Carbohydrates are used by the body as an energy source, and it is important to provide the body with adequate energy from carbohydrate sources. However, the quality of the carbohydrates is important. Examples of high-quality carbohydrate sources are whole-grain products, vegetables, and fruits. With regard to whole-grain products, we recommend quinoa, basmati rice, millet, and barley. Select darker green and colored vegetables and eat them raw or slightly steamed. Fruits are better eaten whole, not as a juice. As with meats, we recommend organic products over highly processed alternatives. A combination of these good carbohydrates will provide your body with adequate energy for exercise and day-to-day activities.

In contrast, bad carbohydrates will drive up insulin levels, increase body fat, and decrease energy levels. In addition, because there is no substantial nutrition from the bad carbohydrates, the body will crave more food, leading to overeating. Examples of these detrimental carbohydrates include candy, pastries, soft drinks, and chips, as well as pasta and breads made with bleached or processed flour.

## EATING SCHEDULE

To keep the body functioning at optimal levels, it is important to keep the blood sugar levels nearly constant (to keep insulin levels from spiking). To achieve this, it is helpful to eat smaller meals more frequently throughout the day (never go longer than three hours without eating). Fill the void between the conventional breakfast, lunch, and dinner schedule with nutritious snacks. Healthy snacks include nuts, fruits, raw vegetables, organic cheese (not processed), and some high protein/low carbohydrate "sports" supplement bars.

## SUPPLEMENTS

If you are eating a nutritious, organic, well-balanced diet, the need for supplements is minimal. However, if your eating habits are typical of most Americans, then you might consider supplements. The supplements we recommend are a quality multimineral multivitamin; liquid essential fatty acids (fish or flax oil); and other high-quality specific supplements that your health care provider might suggest.

# 3-DAY SAMPLE EATING SCHEDULE
## Modified for three different workout times

## DAY 1

LUNCHTIME WORKOUT

7:30 A.M. **BREAKFAST**
16 oz herbal tea
2 scrambled eggs
2 turkey sausage links
Take appropriate supplements.

10:00 A.M. **SNACK**
Peach or banana
3 oz almonds
16 oz water

11:30 A.M. **PREWORKOUT MEAL**
Light salad with tuna or chicken
(raspberry vinaigrette dressing)
16 oz water

12:30 P.M. **WORKOUT**
Sport drink or water during workout

2:30 P.M. **POSTWORKOUT MEAL**
Whey protein with 1% milk or water
(add fruit such as a banana or blueberries if desired)

4:00 P.M. **SNACK**
Protein bar
16 oz water

6:00 P.M. **DINNER**
Salmon and basmati rice
Steamed vegetables
16 oz water
Take nighttime supplements as necessary.

# DAY 2

MORNING WORKOUT

6:00 A.M. **PREWORKOUT MEAL**
16 oz herbal tea
2 eggs and 6 oz cottage cheese
Take appropriate supplements.

7:00 A.M. **WORKOUT**
Sport drink or water during workout

9:00 A.M. **POSTWORKOUT MEAL**
Whey protein drink blended with a banana in
1% milk or water

10:30 A.M. **SNACK**
Pear or apple
3 oz cashews
16 oz water

12:30 P.M. **LUNCH**
Chicken breast (no skin)
Steamed vegetables
Long-grain rice
16 oz water

3:30 P.M. **SNACK**
Low-fat yogurt
16 oz water

6:00 P.M. **DINNER**
Organic fillet (red meat)
Steamed vegetables
Salad (balsamic dressing)
16 oz water
Take nighttime supplements as necessary.

# DAY 3

EVENING WORKOUT

7:30 A.M. **BREAKFAST**
16 oz herbal tea
7-grain breakfast mush
Take appropriate supplements.

10:00 A.M. **SNACK**
Whey protein drink blended with a banana in
1% milk or water

12:00 P.M. **LUNCH**
Buffalo burger (no bun)
Large salad (oil and vinegar dressing)
16 oz water

2:30 P.M. **SNACK**
Cottage cheese and peaches

4:00 P.M. **PREWORKOUT MEAL**
Protein bar
16 oz water

5:00 P.M. **WORKOUT**
Sport drink or water during workout

7:00 P.M. **DINNER**
1–2 chicken breasts (no skin)
Basmati rice
Steamed vegetables
16 oz water
Take nighttime supplements as necessary.

NOTE: *If you are hungry at night, we recommend a low-carbohydrate/high-protein energy bar.*

## Specific Recommendations

| PROTEINS 2–3 X A DAY | VEGETABLES 2–3 X A DAY | GRAINS 1–2 X A DAY | SNACKS 1–2 X A DAY | DRINKS | SUPPLEMENTS | DON'T EAT |
|---|---|---|---|---|---|---|
| Eggs | Broccoli | Quinoa | Fruits | Water | Fiber | Sugars |
| Chicken/turkey | Cauliflower | Millet | Yogurt | Sport | Vitamins | Pasta |
| Fish (salmon) | Squash/ zucchini | Basmati rice | Protein bars | Herbal tea | Liquid minerals | Corn Potatoes |
| Red meat (organic, lean) | Dark greens (salad—**no** iceberg lettuce) | 7–10-grain mush | Nuts (almonds, cashews— **no** salt) | | Calcium and magnesium | Breads White flour Bagels |
| Game (i.e., venison) | Spinach | Flax | | | EFAs | Chips |
| Cottage cheese | Green vegetable powder mix | Long-grain rice | | | Protein powder (whey) | Processed foods |
| Protein powder (whey) Protein bars | | | | | | Excessive dairy |
| | | | | | | Soft drinks |
| | | | | | | Candy |

## IMPORTANCE OF REST

Rest is as critical for your body as good nutrition. Because one of the most common mistakes made with resistive training is overtraining, it is important to understand the necessity of rest and recovery. In resistive training, the muscle tissue *itself* is being broken down. Following the workout, the muscle tissue rebuilds itself, increasing in size and strength. If there is not adequate rest time after a workout, the muscles can't recover, resulting in the continuous breakdown of muscle tissue. This is what we mean by "overtraining."

Another way of overtraining is allowing the workout to last too long. The length of a resistive training workout should be no longer than 60 minutes. After 60 minutes, the muscles lose their energy stores (adenosine triphosphate [ATP], creatine phosphate [CP], and glycogen), greatly diminishing the training efficiency.

If you are doing resistive training four or more times a week, we strongly recommend alternating upper body and lower body workouts, utilizing the BAM (Balanced Antagonistic Muscle) Superset system discussed in the Introduction. The BAM Superset system allows you to achieve maximum results and recovery while minimizing the potential for injury. At a minimum, get at least a day's rest between similar workouts. For more information on this subject, refer to the guidelines in Chapter 11, "Designing Your Own Workout."

To optimize your workout results, a combination of adequate rest, hydration, and high-quality nutrition is absolutely essential. Without these, muscle recovery and the resultant increases in size and strength are significantly thwarted.

# the chapter of lists

THINGS YOU WILL LEARN IN THIS CHAPTER:

**THE "TOP TEN" COMMON MISTAKES**

**LITTLE THINGS MEAN A LOT**

**IMPORTANT LITTLE DETAILS OFTEN OVERLOOKED**

**BENEFITS OF RESISTANCE AND CARDIOVASCULAR TRAINING**

**GYM ETIQUETTE AND BASIC GUIDELINES IN HEALTH CLUBS**

**THE "TOP FIVE" COMMON MYTHS**

**EXERCISES TO AVOID AND WHY**

# the chapter of lists

For this chapter we have compiled several lists, all containing information that we feel is important to know prior to working out in a gym.

| The "Top Ten" Common Mistakes |
|---|
| 1. OVERTRAINING. |
| 2. USING THE ARMS TOO MUCH IN UPPER BODY TRAINING. |
| 3. USING MOMENTUM TO PERFORM THE LIFTS. |
| 4. NOT ISOLATING THE MUSCLES BEING TRAINED (LACK OF FOCUS). |
| 5. USING TOO MUCH OR NOT ENOUGH WEIGHT. |
| 6. USE OF IMPROPER TECHNIQUE. |
| 7. GETTING OUT OF, OR NEVER ACHIEVING, CORRECT POSTURAL ALIGNMENT. |
| 8. DOING TOO MUCH WHEN FIRST STARTING A WORKOUT PROGRAM. |
| 9. NOT STAYING WELL HYDRATED DURING WORKOUTS. |
| 10. INCONSISTENCY IN WORKOUT SCHEDULES. |

## LITTLE THINGS MEAN A LOT

The first list contains information that we feel cannot be overlooked. It is extremely important to pay attention to the details in order to maximize your results.

### IMPORTANT LITTLE DETAILS OFTEN OVERLOOKED

1. **Remember to eat before the workout** as it is important to provide good fuel for your body prior to exercising. This preworkout meal, which typically includes a mix of protein and good carbohydrates, should not be heavy and should be consumed 45 to 60 minutes prior to the workout.

2. **Clothing should be comfortable.** Do not wear jeans or dress shoes. Gym shoes are the preferred footwear. If you have a joint or tendon problem, start the workout wearing warmer clothing that can be removed as you warm up.

3. **Warm up prior to working out.** Don't start the resistive training or intense cardio portion of your workout without first warming up. We recommend starting with five minutes on a stationary bike or treadmill. If you are going to use heavy weights during the workout, include a lighter warm-up set or two before starting the heavy lifting.

4. **Stay hydrated during the workout.** It is very important to stay well hydrated during workouts. Water or various sport drinks are effective.

5. **Breathe during each repetition (rep).** Never hold your breath during weight lifting. Maintain a rhythmic breathing pattern during each rep, typically exhaling

during the push or exertion phase and inhaling during the lengthening or return phase of a rep.

6. **"Work in" with others—share equipment.** If the piece of equipment you want to use is occupied, it is common gym etiquette to ask to "work in." This is a way to share equipment by taking turns doing a set. This works well when both people are using a BAM (Balanced Antagonistic Muscle) Superset training technique.

7. **Do not watch what everybody else does.** This can be a *big* mistake! Approximately 75 percent of people working out in a health club environment are using what we consider to be improper or potentially harmful technique. If you are not careful, you may acquire their bad habits. In addition, just because someone looks good does not mean that the exercise they are doing will be good for you.

8. **Maintain an even pace throughout the workout.** Often people will wait or stand around until a machine is available. If you cannot effectively "work in" on that machine, it is perfectly acceptable—and still effective—to go on to another exercise or BAM Superset, coming back and doing that machine later. It is important to keep going and to limit the down time or social time during a 45- to 60-minute workout.

9. **Make sure you have an even grip or foot placement on a barbell, dumbbell, or machine.** When using dumbbells, make sure to grip in the middle of the bar. Improper foot placement or an uneven hand position will reduce the effectiveness of isolating the muscle group being trained. In addition, it can lead to asymmetric muscle development and reduce your ability to maintain core posture. For additional information, refer to Chapter 3, "Posture and Ergonomics."

**PROPER DUMBBELL GRIP**

**IMPROPER DUMBBELL GRIP**

## Benefits of Resistance and Cardiovascular Training

1. **INCREASED STRENGTH AND MUSCLE ENDURANCE.**
2. **IMPROVED POSTURE.**
3. **REDUCED OR DELAYED OCCURRENCE OF OSTEOPOROSIS.**
4. **INCREASED FLEXIBILITY.**
5. **PREVENTION OF INJURIES.**
6. **FASTER REHABILITATION FROM INJURIES.**
7. **IMPROVED SELF-IMAGE AND CONFIDENCE.**
8. **IMPROVED KINESTHETIC CAPABILITIES.**
9. **REVERSED OR DELAYED AFFECTS OF AGING.**
10. **INCREASED METABOLIC RATE WITH RESULTANT REDUCTION OF OVERALL BODY FAT.**
11. **INCREASED ENERGY.**
12. **REDUCED STRESS.**
13. **REDUCTION OR PREVENTION OF LIFE-THREATENING ILLNESSES.**
14. **INCREASED SELF-AWARENESS.**
15. **IMPROVED SOCIAL LIFE.**

10. **Maintain core posture throughout the entire set.** In order to achieve the optimum result from any exercise, maintaining proper form is of paramount importance. One of the keys to accomplishing this is to maintain core posture during the entire exercise. As explained in Chapter 3, "Posture and Ergonomics," maintaining and understanding core posture is the foundation for achieving proper form and maximum benefit from any exercise.

11. **Stay focused during a set.** It can be easy to let your mind drift during a set, thinking about something that has already happened or what you are planning to do next. This has a dramatic impact on the effectiveness of your effort. As you lose focus, your form deteriorates, and, as a result, the isolation of the muscle(s) being trained is diminished.

12. **Stay focused on correct technique.** Before each exercise, review the correct technique for that exercise. If your form and technique are off, even a little, it can diminish the effectiveness of the exercise. Maintaining correct form and technique throughout the exercise will provide proper targeting of the muscle(s), maximizing the benefit.

13. **Keep an even pace with a fluid movement pattern.** A common error in resistive training is to perform the exercise at a fast pace, utilizing momentum and speed to accomplish the lift. This reduces the effectiveness of the exercise by diminishing the isolation of the muscle being targeted. The preferred pace should be a controlled, fluid movement, generally two to three seconds on the concentric phase (shortening) and two to three seconds on the eccentric phase (lengthening).

14. **Concentrate on the muscles being worked.** Too many people who work out are unsure of exactly what

muscles they are training. Before beginning any exercise, you should be aware of the muscles you are going to train. During the exercise it is extremely important to focus on the muscles being worked and the way that they move. This allows you to achieve maximum isolation of any given muscle or muscle group.

15. **Remember to eat after the workout.** As explained in Chapter 1, muscle tissue is broken down and energy stores are depleted during exercise. Therefore, it is crucial to provide ample proteins and quality carbohydrates to aid muscle tissue recovery and to immediately replenish energy stores. This postworkout meal should be eaten within 30 to 60 minutes of completing the workout.

## Gym Etiquette and Basic Guidelines in Health Clubs

1. **SHARE EQUIPMENT. THIS IS OFTEN REFERRED TO AS "WORKING IN," OR MORE COMMONLY KNOWN AS TAKING TURNS.**

2. **WEAR PROPER WORKOUT ATTIRE INCLUDING COMFORTABLE CLOTHES AND CLOSED-TOE SHOES.**

3. **DO NOT SWEAR.**

4. **WIPE EQUIPMENT AFTER USE IF YOU LEAVE IT SWEATY.**

5. **RERACK YOUR WEIGHTS WHEN FINISHED WITH THEM.**

6. **DON'T DROP/SLAM WEIGHTS OR BE HARSH WITH EQUIPMENT.**

## The "Top Five" Common Myths

1. **WEIGHT TRAINING WILL MAKE YOU "MUSCLE BOUND."**

2. **WEIGHT TRAINING IS ONLY FOR ATHLETES.**

3. **"NO PAIN, NO GAIN."**

4. **IF WOMEN WORK OUT THEY WILL "BULK UP" AND LOOK LIKE A BODYBUILDER.**

5. **WEIGHT TRAINING WILL HINDER SPORT(S) PERFORMANCE.**

## EXERCISES TO AVOID AND WHY

1. **Behind the neck pull downs.**
   This exercise places incredible strain on the cervical spine.

2. **Behind the neck shoulder press.**
   This exercise places strain on the neck and the shoulder joint capsule.

3. **Stiff-legged dead lifts.**
   This exercise places too much strain on the lumbar vertebrae.

4. **Upright rows.**
   This exercise can create or result in shoulder impingement syndrome.

5. **Heavy negatives.**
   Heavy negatives occur when one tries to control too much weight in the eccentric phase of the lift. Generally, this is done when muscles are fatigued and the weight becomes too much to handle on the concentric phase. This creates too great a risk of injury and places too much stress on the tendons and joints.

# posture and ergonomics

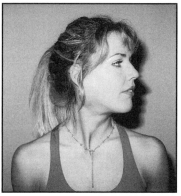

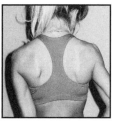

THINGS YOU WILL LEARN IN THIS CHAPTER:

**DEFINING POSTURE**

**MOVING FROM POOR POSTURE TO GOOD POSTURE**

**THREE POINTS TO REMEMBER IN FINDING CORRECT POSTURE**

**BREAKDOWN OF THREE STATIC POSTURE POSITIONS**
   WHILE SITTING IN AN OFFICE CHAIR
   WHILE SITTING ON A SWISS BALL
   WHILE STANDING

**UNDERSTANDING YOUR FOOT CENTERS**

**THE DAILY DOZEN™ EXERCISES**

**PROPER ERGONOMICS AT A COMPUTER WORKSTATION**

# proper posture

## DEFINING POSTURE

When exercising, there are two elements of body positioning that are very important. First, establish a correct overall body alignment or positioning with respect to the machine or free-weight exercise being performed. This is a static postural positioning. In addition, and more important, maintain core posture during the movement itself. This is a dynamic postural integration requiring the use of core stabilizing musculature.

By definition, posture is the body's relationship to gravity and its surroundings. Core posture is the symmetric positioning (maintaining balance) of the body relative to the center of the body. In exercise, and in movement in general, good core posture provides a solid foundation from which to move.

### Definitions

**POSTURE:
THE BODY'S RELATIONSHIP TO GRAVITY AND ITS SURROUNDINGS.**

**CORE POSTURE:
SYMMETRIC POSITIONING (MAINTAINING BALANCE) OF THE BODY RELATIVE TO THE CENTER OF THE BODY.**

## MOVING FROM POOR POSTURE TO GOOD POSTURE

Three examples of poor posture and the stress they place on the body are shown in photos on page 15. By applying the following three effective—yet simple—movements, you can move from poor posture to good posture.

### Moving from Poor Posture to Good Posture

1. **UPLIFT THE STERNUM WHILE ROTATING YOUR SHOULDER BLADES DOWNWARD (ANCHORING).**

2. **ALIGN YOUR PELVIS AND ENGAGE YOUR STOMACH MUSCLES.**

3. **ELONGATE AND CENTER YOUR HEAD AND NECK OVER YOUR SPINE.**

### Three Points to Remember in Finding Correct Posture

1. **CORE POSTURE.**
2. **STERNUM TO SCAPULA RELATIONSHIP.**
3. **PROPER HEAD POSITION.**

## MOVING FROM POOR POSTURE TO GOOD POSTURE

### FIGURE 1

### FIGURE 2

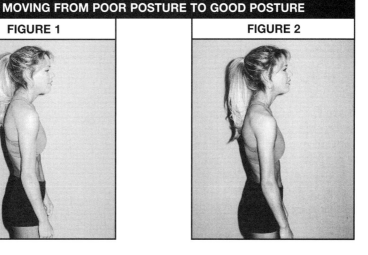

### FIGURE 3

### FIGURE 4

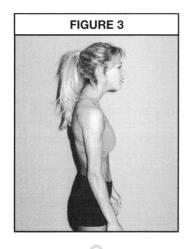

1

This figure shows poor posture with a collapsed sternum. Stress is placed on the neck, shoulders, and upper back.

2

This figure shows poor posture with a flat back (spine) and the head forward. Stress is placed on the neck and lower back.

3

This figure shows poor posture with a "forward head posture." Stress is placed on the lower cervical spine, shoulders, and jaw.

4

This figure shows good posture achieved by applying the three basic principles listed on the previous page. Note that the sternum is uplifted and the head, shoulders, upper back, and pelvis are all in alignment.

# breakdown of three static
## posture positions

### WHILE SITTING IN AN OFFICE CHAIR

1. Keep your feet flat on the ground 8-12 inches apart.
2. Bend your legs at an angle that is slightly greater than 90 degrees.
3. Evenly distribute your body weight over the right and left sides of your hip bones as you sit in the chair.
4. Use a lumbar support for your lower back, while reclined at an angle of 100-110 degrees—not at a 90-degree angle (completely straight up).
5. Uplift and open your chest cavity.
6. Center your head directly over your chest cavity and shoulder blades. Next, think of your neck being uplifted and lengthened up and out from your shoulders without tucking your chin.
7. Think of elevating and lengthening your entire body and spine upward three inches.

### WHILE SITTING ON A SWISS BALL

1. Keep your feet flat on the ground 8-12 inches apart.
2. Bend your legs at 90-degree angles (right angles).
3. Evenly distribute your body weight over the right and left sides of your hip bones as you sit on the Swiss Ball.
4. Engage your lower abs by pulling your belly in toward your spine.
5. Uplift and open your chest cavity.
6. Take your shoulder blades and shoulders back and down (anchor them) without arching your lower back. Your chest cavity should be directly over your hips.
7. Center your head directly over your chest cavity and shoulder blades. Next, think of your neck being uplifted and lengthened up and out from your shoulders without tucking your chin.
8. Think of elevating and lengthening your entire body and spine upward three inches.

## WHILE STANDING

1. Stand with your feet shoulder width apart.
2. Evenly distribute your body weight over both feet. Be aware of any tendency you may have to shift more of your body weight onto one foot.
3. Keep your knees slightly bent, making sure they are not hyperextended.
4. Engage your lower abs by pulling your belly in toward your spine.
5. Uplift and open your chest cavity.
6. Take your shoulder blades and shoulders back and down (anchor them) without arching your lower back. Your chest cavity should be directly over your hips.
7. Center your head directly over your chest cavity and shoulder blades. Next, think of your neck being uplifted and lengthened up and out from your shoulders without tucking your chin.
8. Think of elevating and lengthening your entire body and spine upward three inches.

# understanding your foot centers

Part of maintaining good core posture starts from your feet. How you stand on your feet can determine, in part, how the rest of your body will be positioned. For example, some people have a tendency to roll to the outside of one or both feet. Others either lean back on their heels or forward on the balls of their feet. This uneven weight distribution across the feet will often carry over into walking and running and will even appear during various lower body exercises.

It is important to try to maintain equal weight distribution across all of your major foot centers. As shown in the

illustration below, each foot has three centers of gravity on the sole (bottom of the foot). The first is located just below the big toe on the pad, or ball, of the foot. The second is below the pinky and ring toe on the pad, or ball, of the foot. The third foot center is located in the center of the heel.

When standing, walking, running, or weight lifting, it is important to always be aware of your foot centers and how your body weight is being distributed over these centers of gravity.

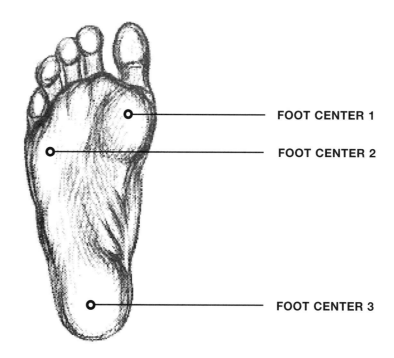

**FOOT CENTER 1**

**FOOT CENTER 2**

**FOOT CENTER 3**

# the daily dozen™
## exercises

The Daily Dozen for a Better Posture exercises are a series of range and motion exercises and stretches that have been designed to improve your overall posture. When performed daily they help to strengthen the muscles of the upper back, shoulders, and neck, which in turn will result in improved posture and posture awareness. Performing the exercises daily will also help to reduce tension in the neck, shoulders, and upper back.

Try doing the Daily Dozen exercises as a warm-up to exercise or yard work. They also are effective as a tension break when working at a computer for extended time periods.

Start off with 12 reps on each of the shoulder and back exercises. Do five reps on each side for the neck and wrist movements. For the upper trap/neck stretch, hold the stretch for 30 seconds on each side. Gradually work up to performing two to three sets of each exercise. These sets can be spread throughout the day.

# exercise one
## finding core posture

**key points**

TAKE YOUR TIME FOLLOWING ALL THE STEPS. MAKE SURE TO USE A MIRROR TO GIVE YOURSELF VISUAL FEEDBACK REGARDING CORRECT BODY POSITION.

**things to avoid**

AVOID RELYING ON YOUR OWN BODY'S PERCEPTION OF WHAT GOOD POSTURE SHOULD BE, AS IT WILL WANT TO GO INTO OLD, INCORRECT POSTURAL HABITS. THIS IS WHY IT IS HELPFUL TO USE A MIRROR.

1. Stand with your feet shoulder width apart.
2. Evenly distribute your body weight over both feet. Be aware of any tendency you may have to shift more of your body weight onto one foot.
3. Keep your knees slightly bent, making sure they are not hyperextended.
4. Engage your lower abs by pulling your belly in toward your spine.
5. Uplift and open your chest cavity.
6. Take your shoulder blades and shoulders back and down (anchor them) without arching your lower back. Your chest cavity should be directly over your hips.
7. Center your head directly over your chest cavity and shoulder blades. Next, think of your neck being uplifted and lengthened up and out from your shoulders without tucking your chin.
8. Think of elevating and lengthening your entire body and spine upward three inches.
9. Once you feel centered and lengthened, engage your abs by pulling your belly straight in toward your spine. You should feel your stomach cavity hollow out. Next, force air out through your mouth as you pull in your abs. Breath in and relax your abs.
10. Now pull the abs in toward the spine for five reps. It is important not to change your core posture position during this exercise.

# reverse circles

| | | |
|---|---|---|
| 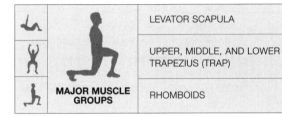 | **MAJOR MUSCLE GROUPS** | LEVATOR SCAPULA |
| | | UPPER, MIDDLE, AND LOWER TRAPEZIUS (TRAP) |
| | | RHOMBOIDS |

**SIDE VIEW**

**key points**

IMAGINE YOU ARE DRAWING CIRCLES WITH YOUR SHOULDERS, MOVING YOUR SHOULDERS WITH YOUR SHOULDER BLADES AND *NOT* YOUR ARMS.

**things to avoid**

AVOID COMPRESSING YOUR HEAD AND NECK. KEEP THEM RELAXED AND LENGTHENED INSTEAD. ROLL SHOULDERS IN FULL AND COMPLETE CIRCLES, IN A COUNTERCLOCKWISE DIRECTION.

**SIDE VIEW**

# exercise three
## reach and pulls

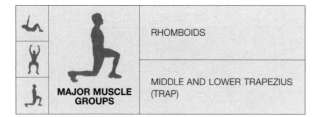

| | RHOMBOIDS |
|---|---|
| **MAJOR MUSCLE GROUPS** | MIDDLE AND LOWER TRAPEZIUS (TRAP) |

1. Begin with your arms extended in front of your body, at chest level.
2. Pull your arms back, using your shoulder blade muscles, until your elbows are in line with your shoulder joints and your arms are at right angles.
3. In the end phase, your palms should be turned up and arms level with the ground, as if carrying a food tray.

**key points**

**UPLIFT AND OPEN UP YOUR CHEST, AS YOU PULL BACK YOUR ARMS USING YOUR SHOULDER BLADES.**

**things to avoid**

**MAKE SURE NOT TO ARCH YOUR BACK; INSTEAD MAINTAIN YOUR CORE POSTURE. AVOID TAKING YOUR ELBOWS PAST YOUR SHOULDER JOINTS AT THE END PHASE.**

**STARTING POSITION, SIDE VIEW**

**END PHASE, SIDE VIEW**

**END PHASE**

# exercise four
## triangles and squares

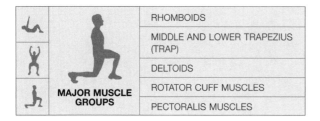

| | | RHOMBOIDS |
|---|---|---|
| | | MIDDLE AND LOWER TRAPEZIUS (TRAP) |
| | **MAJOR MUSCLE GROUPS** | DELTOIDS |
| | | ROTATOR CUFF MUSCLES |
| | | PECTORALIS MUSCLES |

**key points**

**UPLIFT AND OPEN UP YOUR CHEST, AS YOU PULL BACK YOUR ARMS USING YOUR SHOULDER BLADES. THINK OF YOUR ARMS HINGING AROUND YOUR SHOULDER JOINTS, SIMILAR TO A DOUBLE DOOR OPENING UP.**

1. Begin with your arms extended out in front of your body, forming a triangle with your hands, at eye level.
2. Pull your arms back into a box/square shape, using your shoulder blade muscles, until your elbows are in line with your shoulder joints. Your arms should be at right angles, forming a square.
3. In the end phase, your wrists, elbows, and shoulder joints should be in alignment.

**STARTING POSITION, SIDE VIEW**

**things to avoid**

MAKE SURE NOT TO ARCH YOUR BACK, MAINTAINING YOUR CORE POSTURE INSTEAD. AVOID TAKING YOUR ELBOWS PAST YOUR SHOULDER JOINTS AT THE END PHASE.

### END PHASE: BACK VIEW

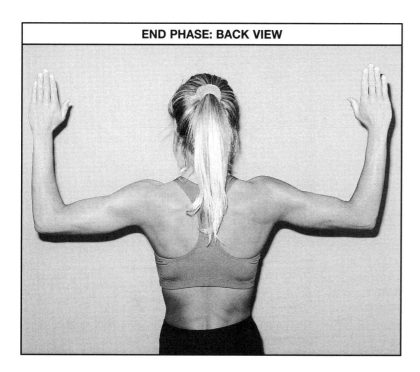

### END PHASE: SIDE VIEW

# front raise and open up to a "w"

**UPLIFT AND OPEN UP YOUR CHEST, AS YOU PULL BACK YOUR ARMS USING YOUR SHOULDER BLADES. THINK OF YOUR ARMS HINGING AROUND YOUR SHOULDER JOINTS, SIMILAR TO A DOUBLE DOOR OPENING UP. ARMS SHOULD MAINTAIN THE "V" POSITION AS THEY ROTATE INTO THE "W" POSITION.**

**things to avoid**

**MAKE SURE NOT TO ARCH YOUR BACK, BUT INSTEAD MAINTAIN YOUR CORE POSTURE. AVOID TAKING YOUR ELBOWS PAST YOUR SHOULDER JOINTS AT THE END PHASE.**

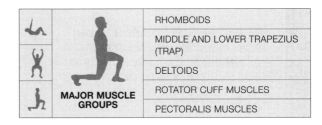

**MAJOR MUSCLE GROUPS**

| |
| --- |
| RHOMBOIDS |
| MIDDLE AND LOWER TRAPEZIUS (TRAP) |
| DELTOIDS |
| ROTATOR CUFF MUSCLES |
| PECTORALIS MUSCLES |

1. Begin with your arms straight and in front of your body.
2. Raise and extend your arms in front of your body, at chest level.
3. Rotate arms into an extended "V" shape. Your wrists, elbows, and shoulders should all be in alignment.
4. Maintaining arms in a "V" position, hinge and rotate arms around the shoulder joints similar to a double door opening up. In the end phase, your arms should form a "W" shape. As you rotate your arms back, make sure that your arms do not move out of the "V" shape position. Focus on moving your arms back using your shoulder blades.

**STARTING POSITION, SIDE VIEW**

**MIDDLE PHASE, SIDE VIEW**

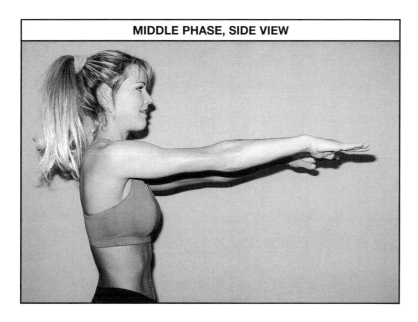

**MIDDLE PHASE, SIDE VIEW**

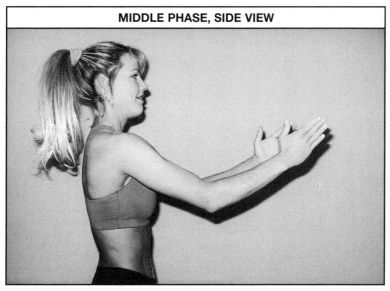

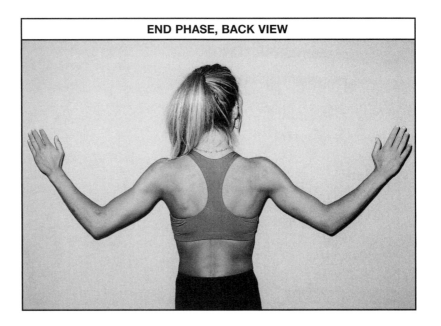

END PHASE, BACK VIEW

# right angle box and open ups

1. Begin with your arms bent at right angles and extended out in front of your body, at chest level.
2. Rotate your arms back into a box/square shape, using your shoulder blade muscles, until your elbows are in line with your shoulder joints. Your arms should remain at right angles, forming a square in the end phase of the movement.
3. In the end phase, your wrists, elbows, and shoulder joints should be in alignment.

| | MAJOR MUSCLE GROUPS | RHOMBOIDS |
| --- | --- | --- |
| | | MIDDLE AND LOWER TRAPEZIUS (TRAP) |
| | | DELTOIDS |
| | | ROTATOR CUFF MUSCLES |
| | | PECTORALIS MUSCLES |

key points

**UPLIFT AND OPEN UP YOUR CHEST, AS YOU PULL BACK YOUR ARMS USING YOUR SHOULDER BLADES. THINK OF YOUR ARMS HINGING AROUND YOUR SHOULDER JOINTS, SIMILAR TO A DOUBLE DOOR OPENING UP.**

things to avoid

**MAKE SURE NOT TO ARCH YOUR BACK, BUT INSTEAD MAINTAIN YOUR CORE POSTURE. AVOID TAKING YOUR ELBOWS PAST YOUR SHOULDER JOINTS AT THE END PHASE.**

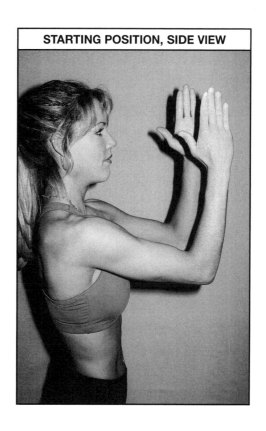

**STARTING POSITION, SIDE VIEW**

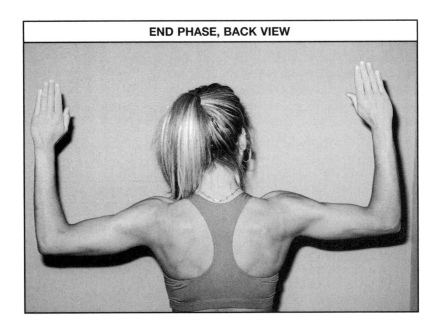

END PHASE, BACK VIEW

# upper body trunk rotations

1. While stretching one arm forward—in line with the center of your body—rotate the opposite arm back, leading with your elbow. Alternate arms and rotations.
2. Think of rotating your body using your torso muscles, without rotating your hips. Arms should flow and not "jam" back.

| | | |
|---|---|---|
| | | OBLIQUES |
| | | ROTATORES OF THE SPINE |
| | **MAJOR MUSCLE GROUPS** | MULTIFIDI OF THE SPINE |

**key points**

ROTATE FROM YOUR TORSO, NOT FROM YOUR HIPS. MAINTAIN A SMOOTH AND FLOWING MOTION.

**things to avoid**

TRY NOT TO SHRUG YOUR SHOULDERS OR FORCE YOUR RANGE OF MOTION.

**FRONT VIEW**

31

**BACK VIEW**

key points

**MAINTAIN YOUR ARMS AT A 90-DEGREE ANGLE AT ALL TIMES.**

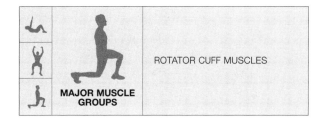

ROTATOR CUFF MUSCLES

**MAJOR MUSCLE GROUPS**

things to avoid

**DO NOT OVEREXTEND YOUR WRISTS OR FORCE YOUR RANGE OF MOTION.**

1. Begin with your elbows at your sides and your arms bent at right angles.
2. Pivot arms around, hinging and rotating at the elbow joints. Rotate arms back comfortably, maintaining a 90-degree arm angle. Keep wrists in line with elbow joints at all times.

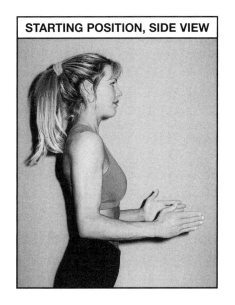

**STARTING POSITION, SIDE VIEW**

**END PHASE**

# exercise nine
## neck rotations

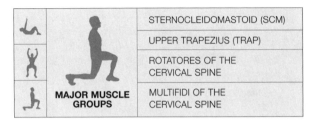

| | | STERNOCLEIDOMASTOID (SCM) |
|---|---|---|
| | | UPPER TRAPEZIUS (TRAP) |
| | | ROTATORES OF THE CERVICAL SPINE |
| | **MAJOR MUSCLE GROUPS** | MULTIFIDI OF THE CERVICAL SPINE |

1. Begin by getting into core posture and having your shoulders level with the ground. Your neck should be relaxed and lengthened.
2. Keeping chin level, rotate your head from right to left, stopping briefly in the middle each time.

**key points**

**MOVE SLOWLY AND WITH CONTROL, KEEPING THE CHIN LEVEL WITH THE GROUND AT ALL TIMES.**

**things to avoid**

**NEVER FORCE YOUR RANGE OF MOTION.**

### STARTING POSITION

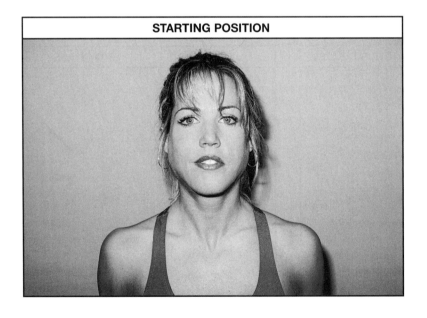

**ROTATION LEFT**

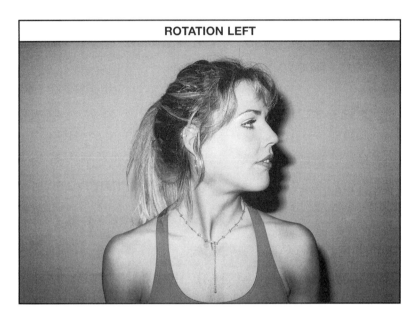

**ROTATION RIGHT**

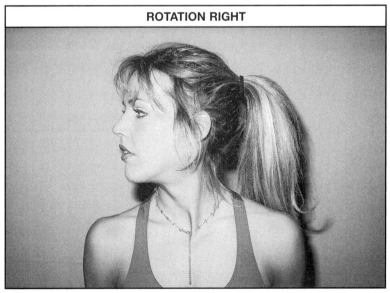

# exercise ten
## lateral neck flexions

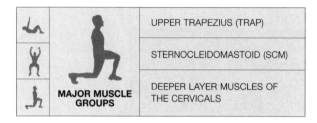

| | | |
|---|---|---|
| | | UPPER TRAPEZIUS (TRAP) |
| | | STERNOCLEIDOMASTOID (SCM) |
| | **MAJOR MUSCLE GROUPS** | DEEPER LAYER MUSCLES OF THE CERVICALS |

1. Begin by getting into core posture, with your shoulders level with the ground. Your neck should be relaxed and lengthened.
2. Laterally bend your head from left to right, stopping briefly in the middle each time.

**key points**

**MOVE SLOWLY AND WITH CONTROL. BEND TO THE SIDE FROM THE UPPER NECK.**

**things to avoid**

**NEVER FORCE YOUR RANGE OF MOTION. DO NOT ROTATE YOUR NECK OR ELEVATE YOUR SHOULDERS.**

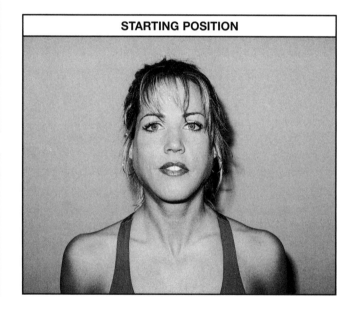

**STARTING POSITION**

**FLEXION LEFT**

**FLEXION RIGHT**

# exercise eleven
## upper trap/neck stretch

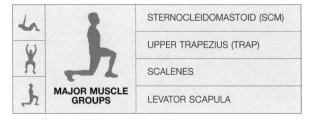

| | | STERNOCLEIDOMASTOID (SCM) |
| --- | --- | --- |
| | | UPPER TRAPEZIUS (TRAP) |
| | | SCALENES |
| | **MAJOR MUSCLE GROUPS** | LEVATOR SCAPULA |

1. Pull one arm across your back to your opposite hip, using your other arm. Hold the arm being stretched at the wrist joint. Stretch your head to the side, in the same direction that you are pulling your arm across.
2. Hold and stretch for 10-15 seconds; then slowly move your head downward and to the side. Find regions that feel tight and hold for 10 seconds before moving on to the next region that is tight. It's important to breath and relax, while maintaining core posture.

key points

**KEEP SHOULDERS AND HIPS LEVEL AT ALL TIMES.**

things to avoid

**DO NOT FORCE THE STRETCH.**

**BACK VIEW**

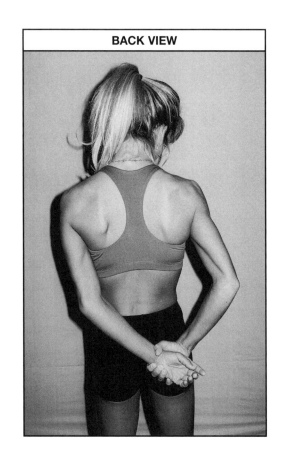

# wrist and forearm stretch

1. Begin with palms touching and forearms level with the ground (if you are very flexible) or slightly above a level plane if your wrists and forearms are tight.
2. Pivot hands from right to left, comfortably stretching your forearms. Do not force range of motion.

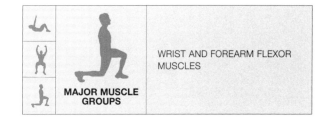

MAJOR MUSCLE GROUPS

WRIST AND FOREARM FLEXOR MUSCLES

**key points**

**IT IS IMPORTANT TO BEND AT THE WRISTS, NOT THE FINGERS.**

**things to avoid**

**DO NOT OVERROTATE FROM THE FINGERS, AND AVOID FORCING THE RANGE OF MOTION.**

| STARTING POSITION | END PHASE |
|---|---|
|  |  |

# proper ergonomics at a
# computer workstation

Working at a computer in any environment, at home or at the office, can place undo stress on the body. The long-term effects of this can lead to serious physical problems. The following photos and guidelines will help you to improve your workplace environment by reducing these stressors. It should be noted that one should take frequent breaks (at a minimum of every hour) and perform various stretches and movement exercises.

## TO ACHIEVE PROPER ERGONOMICS

1. To determine the distance your monitor should be away from your body, fully extend your right arm out. Your fingers should almost touch the center of your screen.
2. The center of the monitor should be 18 degrees below horizontal of your eye level. If using reference material, this material should also be placed at this level. Your monitor and keyboard should be centered with the midline of your body.
3. Your chair should have good lumbar support and should be reclined at an angle of 100 to 110 degrees—not at an upright angle of 90 degrees.

**PROPER DISTANCE FROM MONITOR**

**RELATIVE POSITION OF CHAIR AND MONITOR**

4. The height of your chair should allow your feet to rest flat on the floor. In addition, the chair's height should allow your legs to bend at a 90-degree angle (or greater) at the knee joint.

5. Your elbows and upper arms should be relaxed and close to the body when typing or using your mouse. The elbow angle should be at or slightly greater than a 90-degree angle.

6. It is important to use a negative tilt keyboard and mouse tray. This helps reduce the stress that is placed on the wrists, elbows, and shoulders when using a keyboard. A negative tilt also allows for the wrists to be in a neutral position, not overextended or overflexed.

7. If using a wrist pad, it important that only the heels of your hands touch the pad. Your wrists should not rest on the pad. This will help avoid any unnecessary compression or pressure on wrist nerves.

**CHAIR HEIGHT ADJUSTMENT**

**CORRECT HAND AND FOREARM POSITIONING**

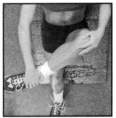

THINGS YOU WILL LEARN IN THIS CHAPTER:

**UPPER TRAP/NECK STRETCH**

**ONE-LEGGED HAMSTRING STRETCH ON THE FLAT BENCH**

**PSOAS/HIP FLEXOR STRETCH**

**GLUTE AND PIRIFORMIS STRETCH**

**LAT STRETCH**

**CHEST STRETCH**

# stretching

Although we only highlight six stretches in this chapter, there are many other options and variations. The stretches we have included cover most of the body's major muscle groups. These stretches should be done periodically throughout the exercise routine (stretching the muscles being trained) and at the end of the session. However, they may also be done throughout the day or following cardiovascular training.

To obtain the most benefit from stretching, the muscles should be warmed up and the stretches should be held for between 30 and 40 seconds. The stretch should not be forced, and breathing should be relaxed during the stretch.

For a good reference on additional stretches, we recommend Bob and Jean Anderson's book, *Stretching,* published by Shelter Publications.

# upper trap/ neck stretch

| | | |
|---|---|---|
| 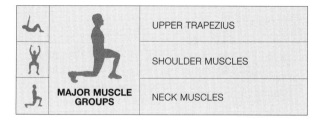 | **MAJOR MUSCLE GROUPS** | UPPER TRAPEZIUS |
| | | SHOULDER MUSCLES |
| | | NECK MUSCLES |

**This is a good stretch if you are experiencing neck and shoulder tightness. It is also a good stretch for people who spend extended periods of time working at a computer.**

## BACK VIEW

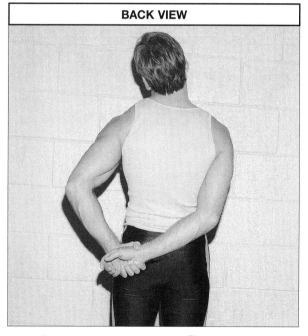

**key points**

**KEEP SHOULDERS AND HIPS LEVEL.**

**things to avoid**

**AVOID FORCING THE STRETCH, ELEVATING THE SHOULDERS OR SHRUGGING, AND BENDING SIDEWAYS AT THE HIP.**

**1**

With hands behind your back, grasp one wrist and pull across to the opposite hip. At the same time, laterally bend the head and neck to that same side.

**2**

Hold the stretch for 30 to 40 seconds on each side, remembering to breathe at all times.

# one-legged hamstring stretch
## on the flat bench

This is an effective hamstring stretch that doesn't put pressure on the lower back. It can be done periodically during a lower body exercise routine.

| | HAMSTRINGS |
| --- | --- |
| **MAJOR MUSCLE GROUPS** | GASTROCNEMIUS (CALVES) |

SIDE VIEW

**key points**

KEEP THE BACK STRAIGHT, THE TOES POINTED UP, AND THE LEG FLAT ON THE BENCH DURING THIS STRETCH.

**things to avoid**

AVOID FORCING THE STRETCH, ROUNDING THE BACK, AND ROTATING THE SHOULDERS OR HIPS.

## 1

Position the leg to be stretched on the bench such that the foot and Achilles tendon are just off the end of the bench. The other leg should be on the floor with the hips and shoulders square and the back straight (no rounding of the spine).

## 2

With the hands at the sides of the bench, bend forward from the waist, maintaining a straight back. It is important to point the toes of the leg being stretched back toward the chest and to keep the leg flat on the bench (do not let the knee bend).

## 3

Hold the stretch for 30 to 40 seconds on each leg, remembering to breathe at all times.

# psoas/hip flexor stretch

| | | |
|---|---|---|
|   | **MAJOR MUSCLE GROUPS** | PSOAS (HIP FLEXORS) |
| | | QUADRICEPS |

This is a great stretch for tight psoas muscles. It is also a good stretch for tight quadricep muscles. It can be done periodically during a lower body exercise routine.

## SIDE VIEW

**key points**

KEEP THE HIPS AND SHOULDERS SQUARE, ANCHOR THE KNEE, AND MOVE THE BODY FORWARD AS A SINGLE UNIT.

**things to avoid**

AVOID FORCING THE STRETCH, ROTATING THE SHOULDERS AND HIPS, AND COLLAPSING THE STERNUM.

**1**

Position one knee on the ground (use a mat or pillow for that knee) and the other leg in front of the body with the knee at a right angle. Align the knee, hip, and shoulder vertically. It is important that the hips and shoulders are square, not rotated.

**2**

Keeping the "down" knee anchored, move the entire body forward as a single unit, leaning forward with the front knee. Accentuate the stretch by uplifting and elongating the stomach and chest. This will increase the stretch in the upper attachments of the psoas muscles.

**3**

Hold the stretch for 30 to 40 seconds on each leg, remembering to breathe at all times.

# glute and piriformis stretch

**This is the best stretch if you have lower back or sciatic-like pain.**

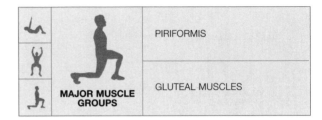

| | PIRIFORMIS |
|---|---|
| **MAJOR MUSCLE GROUPS** | GLUTEAL MUSCLES |

**key points**

KEEP THE LEG AT A RIGHT ANGLE, CRADLING IT ACROSS THE BODY TO THE OPPOSITE SHOULDER.

**things to avoid**

AVOID FORCING THE STRETCH AND ROTATING THE HIPS OR THE OPPOSITE LEG.

### TOP VIEW

### BOTTOM VIEW

**1**

Lying on your back, cradle one leg at the knee and ankle (leg should be bent at a right angle) and pull the bent leg across the body to the opposite shoulder. To enhance the stretch, you can pull up on the ankle and push out on the knee.

**2**

During the stretch, keep the opposite leg straight with foot straight up (not rotated). It is also important to keep the back and hips flat on the ground.

**3**

Hold the stretch for 30 to 40 seconds on each leg, remembering to breathe at all times.

# lat
## stretch

| | | |
|---|---|---|
|  |  | LATISSIMUS DORSI |
| | | MAJOR BACK MUSCLES |
| | **MAJOR MUSCLE GROUPS** | |

**This is the best single upper body stretch available. When done properly, it hits from the shoulders down through the lower back (lumbodorsal fascia). It is very effective when done throughout an upper body workout.**

### BACK VIEW

**key points**

**KEEP THE BACK FLAT, PULL BACK WITH YOUR BODY WEIGHT INTO THE HIPS, AND BOW OUT THE SHOULDER AND ARMPIT HORIZONTALLY.**

**things to avoid**

**AVOID FORCING THE STRETCH, ROUNDING THE BACK, AND ROTATING THE SHOULDERS OR HIPS.**

**1**

Find a stationary object that you can hold on to at stomach level. Face the object standing approximately 3 to 4 feet away. Grasp the object with one hand.

**2**

Align the same side foot with the grasping hand and squat back and down such that the back is flat like a table and the hand, shoulder, and same side hip are in alignment. Pull back with the hips, creating an elongated spine, and follow immediately with shifting the shoulder and armpit horizontally outward.

**3**

Hold the stretch for 30 to 40 seconds on each side, remembering to breathe at all times.

# chest stretch

This is an effective stretch for the chest that can be done periodically during an upper body exercise routine.

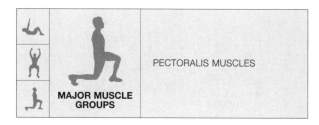

PECTORALIS MUSCLES

MAJOR MUSCLE GROUPS

**STEP INTO THE STRETCH, KEEPING THE SHOULDERS DOWN AND THE ELBOW BENT. KEEP THE STERNUM UPLIFTED AT ALL TIMES.**

**AVOID FORCING THE STRETCH, ELEVATING THE SHOULDER OR SHRUGGING, STRAIGHTENING THE ARM, AND OVERROTATING THE SHOULDERS AND HIPS.**

FRONT VIEW

## 1

Using a doorway or a solid object, position a hand at shoulder height with palm forward. Keeping the arm slightly bent and the sternum uplifted, step forward into the stretch, keeping the hips and shoulders square (don't rotate in the torso).

## 2

To increase the stretch on the chest, you can step forward a little further and slightly rotate the shoulders and hips together in the opposite direction of the side being stretched.

## 3

Hold the stretch for 30 to 40 seconds on each side, remembering to breathe at all times.

# the chest muscles

# chapter five

THINGS YOU WILL LEARN IN THIS CHAPTER:

**CYBEX® VR-2 CHEST PRESS**

**DUMBBELL INCLINE PRESS**

**PEC-DEC FLY**

**CABLE CROSSOVERS**

**FLAT BENCH PRESS**

**INCLINE BENCH PRESS**

# the chest
## muscles

The chest and arm muscles are the focus of most individuals' upper body training program. Unfortunately, this type of training program often leads to overtraining, upper body imbalances, and shoulder problems. For this reason, we recommend that the chest and back be trained together using the BAM Superset training technique. This technique helps to create symmetry in the upper body and reduces the chances of shoulder and neck problems.

To effectively isolate and train the chest muscles, you must first be able to anchor your shoulders. This is accomplished by training the upper back muscles. Once you have learned to retract and anchor your shoulder blades without compensating with your arms and upper traps or collapsing the sternum, you can effectively isolate and train your chest muscles. In addition, this shoulder anchoring helps to alleviate shoulder impingement syndrome (compression and pressure on the supraspinatus and bicepital tendons), which is often a problem when working the chest muscles.

This chapter includes six effective chest exercises. Several of these can be combined in BAM Supersets with exercises listed in Chapter 6, "The Upper Back Muscles." For additional examples of BAM Superset exercise combinations, see Chapter 11, "Designing Your Own Workout." We recommend that you do not perform either the bench or incline bar press until you have developed a strong, balanced upper body muscle base.

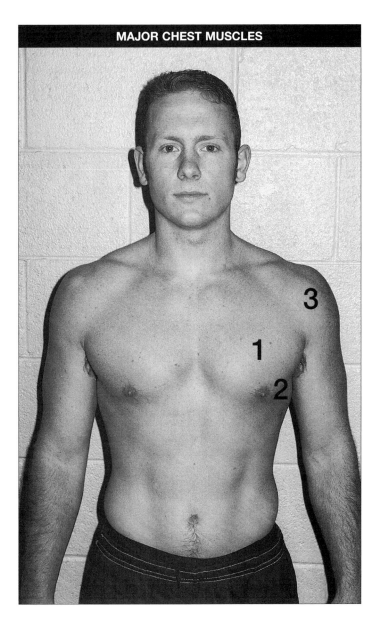

**MAJOR CHEST MUSCLES**

## 1

**PECTORALIS MUSCLES (CHEST)**

## 2

**SERRATUS ANTERIOR**

## 3

**ANTERIOR DELTOID**

# cybex® vr-2 chest press

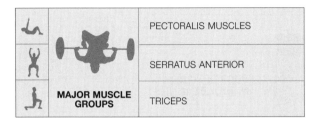

| | | PECTORALIS MUSCLES |
| --- | --- | --- |
| | | SERRATUS ANTERIOR |
| | **MAJOR MUSCLE GROUPS** | TRICEPS |

**This versatile Cybex® machine provides the ability to do both beginning and advanced level movements. The advanced move is excellent for exposing any strength imbalances that may exist in the upper body and, when performed properly, is easily the most effective exercise for isolating the chest muscles.**

| BEGINNING PHASE ▶ ▶ ▶ | END PHASE/LESS CHALLENGING ▶ |
| --- | --- |

### 1
Adjust seat to the proper position. Proper positioning aligns the handles with the upper third of the chest. Set handles in a position that does not produce too much strain on your shoulder joints in the starting position.

### 2
Using an overhand grip, grip the handles in the middle or extended out as wide as possible.

### 3
Begin with the sternum/chest uplifted, tighten the abs, and do not arch the lower back. Shoulders and elbows should be dropped down (arms at 70 degrees in the abduction plane).

### 4
To start the movement, uplift the chest while dropping/rotating the shoulder blades down and back (anchored). Initiate movement with the outer chest muscles. For a less challenging movement,* push straight out and up (as

**key points**

**KEEP THE CHEST UP
AND THE SHOULDERS
AND ELBOWS DOWN.**

**things to avoid**

**AVOID UPLIFTING THE ELBOWS
AND SHRUGGING THE
SHOULDERS OR NECK.**

**END PHASE/MORE CHALLENGING**

**BEGINNING PHASE INCORRECT**

5

in the second picture). For a more challenging movement, move arms in a "V" motion until they are fully extended, bringing both handles together, touching at the end phase of the movement (as in the third picture).

In both movements, the shoulders should remain anchored (down and back) while keeping the chest constantly uplifted. Focus on using the muscles of the chest.

*With any chest press machine, you may implement the same technique as listed in step 4 for the less challenging, straight press-out movement (see the first and second pictures).

# dumbbell
## incline press

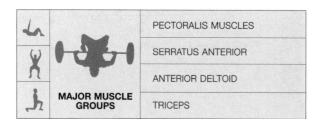

| | | PECTORALIS MUSCLES |
|---|---|---|
| | | SERRATUS ANTERIOR |
| | | ANTERIOR DELTOID |
| | **MAJOR MUSCLE GROUPS** | TRICEPS |

**A good power and strength move, the dumbbell incline press also involves muscle coordination and challenges the muscular stabilization of the shoulder joint. The incline press is preferred over the flat bench press because it puts less strain on the neck, shoulders, and lower back.**

| BEGINNING PHASE/SIDE VIEW ▶▶ | BEGINNING PHASE/SIDE VIEW INCORRECT ▶ |
|---|---|

### 1
Adjust the bench to a 30-degree angle.

### 2
Take an even grip on the dumbbells (in the middle of the dumbbell).

### 3
Begin with the sternum/chest uplifted, tighten the abs, and do not arch the lower back. Dumbbells should be positioned just above the armpit cavities. Dumbbell starting position should be such that dumbbells are in a horizontal straight line with one another and the wrists and weights should be in line over the elbows. Initiate the movement with the chest muscles. Move arms in an arclike motion until arms are fully extended with the dumbbells 1 inch apart. At the end phase the dumbbells should be in line above the mouth.

## ▶ BEGINNING PHASE/FRONT VIEW

4

During the entire movement, the shoulders should remain anchored (down and back), while keeping the chest constantly uplifted.

Focus on using the muscles of the chest.

| key points | KEEP THE CHEST OPEN, THE SHOULDERS ANCHORED DOWN, AND THE WRISTS AND ELBOWS ALIGNED UNDER THE DUMBBELLS AT ALL TIMES. | things to avoid | AVOID COLLAPSING THE STERNUM/CHEST AND MOVING THE WEIGHTS AND FOREARMS OUT OF VERTICAL ALIGNMENT WITH THE ELBOWS. |
|---|---|---|---|

## ▶ END PHASE/SIDE VIEW

## ▶ ▶ ▶ END PHASE/FRONT VIEW

# pec-dec fly

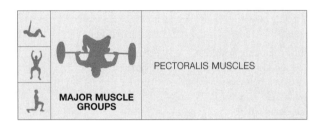

| | |
|---|---|
| | PECTORALIS MUSCLES |
| **MAJOR MUSCLE GROUPS** | |

**This is not a power move, but an effective isolator of the chest muscles. Caution should be exercised when doing this exercise if one has shoulder problems.**

| FRONT PHASE ▶ ▶ ▶ | BACK PHASE ▶ |
|---|---|

**1**

Adjust the seat such that the hands grip at the same level as the upper third of the chest. In the starting position the arms should be bent in a "V" position with the elbows pointing straight down and the thumbs lined up with the top of the shoulder joint.

**2**

Take your arms back until they line up with the middle of your body. Arms should be in the shape of a giant "W" with the elbows pointing down. Wrists, elbows, and shoulder joints should all be in line. To return to the starting position, initiate movement with the chest muscles and continue using only the chest muscles until completion of the movement (the tendency is to use the arms and biceps rather than the chest).

**key points**

MAINTAIN A "V" SHAPE IN THE ARMS AND HINGE AT THE SHOULDER JOINT.

**things to avoid**

AVOID MOVING THE ELBOWS OUT OF ALIGNMENT WITH THE WRISTS AND SHOULDERS.
A COMMON MISTAKE IS TO SHRUG THE SHOULDERS AND ROTATE THE ELBOWS BEHIND THE SHOULDER JOINTS.

**BACK PHASE INCORRECT**

# cable
## crossovers

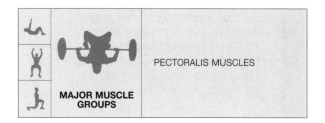

PECTORALIS MUSCLES

**MAJOR MUSCLE GROUPS**

This is not a power move, but an effective isolator of the chest muscles. Caution should be exercised when doing this exercise if one has shoulder problems.

**FRONT PHASE** ▶

1

In the starting position, arms should be bent in a "V" position with the elbows pointing straight down and the hands facing each other and lined up with the middle of the chest.

key points

**FOCUS ON PERFORMING THE MOVEMENT FROM THE CHEST MUSCLES, NOT THE ARMS, KEEPING THE STERNUM UPLIFTED AT ALL TIMES.**

things to avoid

**AVOID MOVING THE ELBOWS OUT OF ALIGNMENT WITH THE WRISTS AND SHOULDERS. A COMMON MISTAKE IS TO SHRUG THE SHOULDERS AND ROTATE THE ELBOWS BEHIND THE SHOULDER JOINTS.**

▶ **BACK PHASE**

2

Take your arms back until they line up with the middle of your body. Arms should be in the shape of a giant "W" with the elbows pointing down. Wrists, elbows, and shoulder joints should all be in line with the hands at the level of the shoulder joint. To return to the starting position, initiate movement with the chest muscles and continue using only the chest muscles until completion of the movement (the tendency is to use the arms and biceps rather than the chest).

# flat bench press

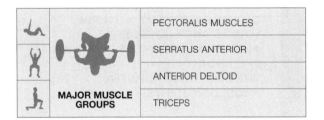

| | | PECTORALIS MUSCLES |
|---|---|---|
| | | SERRATUS ANTERIOR |
| | | ANTERIOR DELTOID |
| | **MAJOR MUSCLE GROUPS** | TRICEPS |

The "king," or benchmark, of upper body strength, this is a great upper body power move. Caution should be exercised if one has lower back, upper back, neck, or shoulder problems.

| ▶ BEGINNING PHASE ▶ ▶ ▶ | MIDDLE PHASE |
|---|---|

## 1

Begin by lining up the eyes under the bar. Take an even hand grip about 4 inches wider than the shoulders (use the knurling mark found on most bars as your reference).

## 2

Begin by lifting the bar off of the rack. Inhale as you lower the bar, under control, to the middle of the chest (nipple line). Upper arms should be between 60 and 70 degrees in the abduction plane with elbows symmetrical.

key points

**MAINTAIN A CONSTANT AND CONTROLLED MOVEMENT OF THE BAR, COMING DOWN TO THE MIDDLE OF THE CHEST WITH EACH REPETITION.**

things to avoid

**AVOID LIFTING THE HIPS OFF OF THE BENCH AND OVERARCHING THE LOWER BACK. AVOID SQUIRMING AND TWISTING THE BODY DURING THE LIFT. WE *STRONGLY* ADVISE USING A SPOTTER DURING THE FLAT BENCH PRESS!**

| BOTTOM PHASE/SIDE VIEW ▶ ▶ ▶ | BOTTOM PHASE/TOP VIEW |

3

Begin pressing the bar up while exhaling and keeping a constant and even push until full extension of the arms is achieved. It is important to note that this is not a straight up movement but an arclike movement from the middle of the chest to above the shoulders.

# incline
## bench press

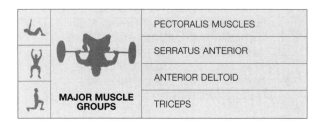

| | | PECTORALIS MUSCLES |
|---|---|---|
| | | SERRATUS ANTERIOR |
| | | ANTERIOR DELTOID |
| | **MAJOR MUSCLE GROUPS** | TRICEPS |

This is a tremendous power move, great for developing upper chest mass. It is preferred over the flat bench press if you have neck or lower back problems.

▶ **BEGINNING PHASE**

1

Adjust the seat height so that eyes are lined up under the bar. Take an even hand grip about 4 inches wider than the shoulders (use the knurling mark found on most bars as your reference).

**key points**

MAINTAIN A CONSTANT AND CONTROLLED MOVEMENT OF THE BAR, COMING DOWN TO THE UPPER CHEST WITH EACH REPETITION.

**things to avoid**

AVOID LIFTING THE HIPS OFF OF THE BENCH AND OVERARCHING THE LOWER BACK. AVOID SQUIRMING AND TWISTING THE BODY DURING THE LIFT. WE *STRONGLY* ADVISE USING A SPOTTER DURING THE INCLINE BENCH PRESS!

| MIDDLE PHASE | ▶ ▶ ▶ | BOTTOM PHASE |
| --- | --- | --- |

## 2

Begin by lifting the bar off of the rack. Inhale as you lower the bar, under control, to the upper chest (second rib). Elbows should be directly under the wrists and the bar.

## 3

Begin pressing the bar up while exhaling and keeping a constant and even push until full extension of the arms is achieved. The bar should move in a straight line, up and down.

# the upper back muscles

# chapter six

THINGS YOU WILL LEARN IN THIS CHAPTER:

**HAMMER STRENGTH® ISO-LATERAL FRONT PULLDOWNS**

**STANDARD LAT FRONT PULLDOWNS**

**CLOSE GRIP FRONT PULLDOWNS**

**CYBEX® ROW**

**SEATED CABLE ROW**

**ONE-ARM DUMBBELL ROW**

# the upper back
## muscles

Heavily interrelated with the shoulders, shoulder blades, and arms, the upper back muscles are some of the most important muscles in upper body posture and shoulder stabilization. Unfortunately, most people working out in a health club or gym do not effectively isolate their upper back muscles. This is because most people dominate movements intended to strengthen the upper back with their arms (pulling arms too far back) and upper traps (shrugging).

To effectively isolate the upper back muscles, it is important to learn first how to move your shoulder blades. There are two primary ways to move the shoulder blades. The first is retraction, or squeezing them together, which involves the rhomboids and middle traps. The second is a downward rotation that involves the lower traps, latissimus dorsi, and teres major muscles. We refer to this as "anchoring the shoulder blades."

Once you have learned to retract and anchor your shoulder blades without compensating with your arms and upper traps or collapsing the sternum, you can effectively isolate and train your upper back muscles. A key element to facilitate these scapular movements is the ability to simultaneously open the chest and uplift the sternum. Because of the interrelation between the sternum/chest muscles and the shoulder blades, we recommend training the upper back and chest muscles together using the BAM Superset technique.

This chapter includes six effective upper back exercises that can be combined in BAM Supersets with the exercises listed in Chapter 5, "The Chest Muscles." See Chapter 11, "Designing Your Own Workout," for examples of exercises to combine in BAM Supersets.

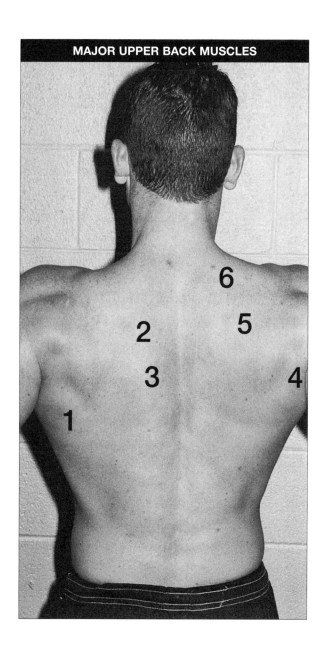

**MAJOR UPPER BACK MUSCLES**

1

**LATISSIMUS DORSI (LATS)**

2

**MIDDLE TRAPEZIUS (TRAPS)**

3

**LOWER TRAPEZIUS (TRAPS)**

4

**TERES MAJOR**

5

**RHOMBOIDS**

6

**UPPER TRAPEZIUS (TRAPS)**

# hammer strength®
## iso-lateral front pulldowns

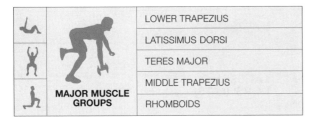

| | | LOWER TRAPEZIUS |
|---|---|---|
| | | LATISSIMUS DORSI |
| | | TERES MAJOR |
| | | MIDDLE TRAPEZIUS |
| | **MAJOR MUSCLE GROUPS** | RHOMBOIDS |

**This is the most effective exercise for isolating the lower traps while minimizing strain on the lower back and neck. The lower traps are a key muscle group for correcting shoulder and postural problems.**

| BEGINNING PHASE ▶ ▶ ▶ | END PHASE/FRONT VIEW ▶ |
|---|---|

### NOTE

This exercise can be performed one arm at a time. The arm not being worked remains up until the other arm completes a full repetition (beginning phase to end phase and back to beginning phase).

**1**
Adjust the seat to the proper position.

**2**
Using an underhand grip, grip at the bend in the bar. If you have smaller hands, use an underhand grip in front of the bend in the bar.

**3**
Begin with the sternum/chest uplifted, tighten the abs, and do not arch the lower back.

**4**
To start the movement, uplift the chest while dropping/rotating the shoulder blades down and back (anchored).

**5**
Drive the elbows straight down. Focus on using the muscles of the shoulder blades, not the arms.

| ► END PHASE/SIDE VIEW | ► ► ► END PHASE/BACK VIEW |

**END PHASE INCORRECT**

## 6

At the end phase of the movement, the sternum/chest should be uplifted and the shoulders should be anchored down and back. The upper arms should be vertical.

## 7

During the entire movement the upper body should remain upright, in good core posture (no arching or leaning back).

**key points**

**KEEP THE CHEST UPLIFTED AND INITIATE MOVEMENT FROM THE SHOULDER BLADES. ANCHOR THE SHOULDERS AT THE BOTTOM PHASE.**

**things to avoid**

**AVOID PULLING THE ELBOWS BACK TOO FAR OR SHRUGGING THE SHOULDERS OR NECK.**

# standard lat front pulldowns

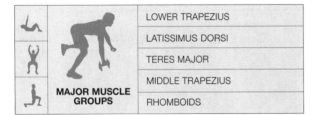

| | | LOWER TRAPEZIUS |
| --- | --- | --- |
| | | LATISSIMUS DORSI |
| | | TERES MAJOR |
| | | MIDDLE TRAPEZIUS |
| | **MAJOR MUSCLE GROUPS** | RHOMBOIDS |

**This is a great upper back power and strength exercise effective in isolating the lats and lower traps. Caution should be exercised when doing this exercise if you have neck problems.**

| BEGINNING PHASE/SIDE VIEW ▶ ▶ ▶ | END PHASE/SIDE VIEW ▶ |
| --- | --- |

## 1
Sit with knees comfortably under the thigh pad.

## 2
Grip the wide bar approximately 3 inches outside your shoulder width.

## 3
Lean back 5 to 10 degrees.

## 4
To start the movement, uplift the chest while dropping/ rotating the shoulder blades down and back (anchored). Pull the bar straight down to the level of the first or second rib (just below your collar bones), no farther.

<table>
<tr></tr>
</table>

| key points | KEY POINTS | things to avoid | THINGS TO AVOID |
|---|---|---|---|

**key points**

**KEEP THE CHEST UPLIFTED AND OPEN, INITIATING MOVEMENT FROM THE SHOULDER BLADES. ANCHOR THE SHOULDERS AT THE BOTTOM PHASE.**

**things to avoid**

**AVOID PULLING THE ELBOWS BACK TOO FAR OR SHRUGGING THE SHOULDERS OR NECK. AVOID ROCKING BACKWARD OR FORWARD AT THE HIP JOINT.**

▶ **END PHASE/BACK VIEW**

▶ ▶ **END PHASE/BACK VIEW INCORRECT**

5

Drive the elbows straight down. Focus on using the muscles of the shoulder blades and back, not the arms.

6

At the end phase of the movement, the sternum/chest should be uplifted to meet the bar and the shoulders should be anchored down and back.

**NOTE**

Note incorrect positioning in the fourth picture. The shoulders are shrugged. The upper traps are engaged while the lats and lower traps are significantly disengaged. This pull missed the target muscles to be worked in this exercise. Compare the third and the fourth pictures. Notice the neck compression in the fourth picture and the degree of contraction of the lats in the third picture as compared to the fourth.

# close grip front pulldowns

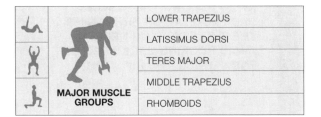

| MAJOR MUSCLE GROUPS | LOWER TRAPEZIUS |
| | LATISSIMUS DORSI |
| | TERES MAJOR |
| | MIDDLE TRAPEZIUS |
| | RHOMBOIDS |

**This exercise provides a great combination of the pulldown and row movements. Precise technique is required for this lift to be effective.**

| BEGINNING PHASE/SIDE VIEW ▶▶▶ | END PHASE/SIDE VIEW ▶ |

**1**

Sit with knees comfortably under the thigh pad.

**2**

Grip with an even grip in the middle of the handles.

**3**

Lean back 5 to 10 degrees.

**4**

To start the movement, uplift the chest while dropping/rotating the shoulder blades down and back (anchored). Pull the handles straight down to the upper chest, no farther.

**KEEP THE CHEST UPLIFTED AND OPEN, INITIATING MOVEMENT FROM THE SHOULDER BLADES. ANCHOR THE SHOULDERS AT THE BOTTOM PHASE.**

**AVOID PULLING THE ELBOWS BACK TOO FAR OR SHRUGGING THE SHOULDERS OR NECK. AVOID ROCKING BACKWARD OR FORWARD AT THE HIP JOINT.**

▶ END PHASE/BACK VIEW

▶▶ END PHASE/BACK VIEW INCORRECT

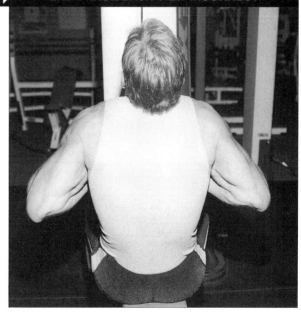

## 5

Drive the elbows straight down. Lift and open the chest into the pull. Focus on using the muscles of the shoulder blades and back, not the arms.

## 6

At the end phase of the movement, the sternum/chest should be uplifted to meet the handles, and the shoulders should be anchored down and back.

**NOTE**

Note incorrect positioning in the fourth picture. The shoulders are shrugged and the back is rounded. The elbows are pulled too far back and are too wide. The upper traps are engaged while the lats and lower traps are significantly disengaged. This pull missed the target muscles to be worked in this exercise. Compare the third and fourth pictures. Notice the neck compression in the fourth picture and the degree of contraction of the lats in the third picture as compared to the fourth.

# cybex®
## row

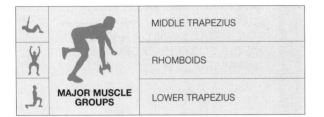

| | | |
|---|---|---|
| | | MIDDLE TRAPEZIUS |
| | | RHOMBOIDS |
| | **MAJOR MUSCLE GROUPS** | LOWER TRAPEZIUS |

**This is a solid and foundational upper back exercise. It is one of the key exercises to be used in overcoming postural problems.**

| BEGINNING PHASE/SIDE VIEW ▶ ▶ ▶ | END PHASE/SIDE VIEW ▶ |
|---|---|

**1**

Adjust the seat and chest pad to proper positions.

**2**

Begin with the sternum/chest uplifted, tighten the abs, and do not arch the lower back. Maintain a core, upright posture during the entire movement.

**3**

Grasp with an even grip on the lower third of the vertical handles. Arms should be fully extended. Avoid excessive forward shoulder rotation.

**4**

Begin by uplifting and opening the chest cavity while squeezing the shoulder blades together. Continue the pull until the upper arms are vertical.

**KEEP THE CHEST UPLIFTED AND OPEN, INITIATING MOVEMENT FROM THE SHOULDER BLADES. SQUEEZE THE SHOULDER BLADES TOGETHER AT THE END PHASE.**

**AVOID USING THE ARM MUSCLES, WINGING OUT THE ELBOWS, AND COLLAPSING THE CHEST (THIS INHIBITS SHOULDER BLADE MOVEMENT). MAKE SURE THE ELBOWS ARE NOT PULLED TOO FAR BACK IN THE FINAL PHASE.**

▶ **END PHASE/BACK VIEW**

5

In the final position the shoulder blades should be fully retracted (pulled toward each other), the upper chest should be uplifted and open, and the shoulders should be rolled down and back.

# seated cable row

This is a solid and foundational upper back exercise and a key exercise that can be used in overcoming postural problems. If you have lower back problems, a machine row, like the Cybex® Row, may be a better option.

| BEGINNING PHASE/SIDE VIEW ▶ | ▶ BEGINNING PHASE/SIDE VIEW INCORRECT ▶ |
|---|---|

### 1
Grasp the handle with an even grip. Start with the legs slightly bent and arms fully extended. Avoid bending forward at the waist.

### 2
Begin with the sternum/chest uplifted, tighten the abs, and do not arch the lower back. Maintain a core, upright posture during the entire movement.

### 3
Begin the movement by uplifting and opening the chest cavity while squeezing the shoulder blades together. Continue the pull until the upper arms are vertical.

### 4
In the final position, the shoulder blades should be fully retracted (pulled toward each other), the upper chest should be uplifted and open, and the shoulders should be rolled down and back (anchored).

▶ **END PHASE/SIDE VIEW**

▶ ▶ **END PHASE/SIDE VIEW INCORRECT**

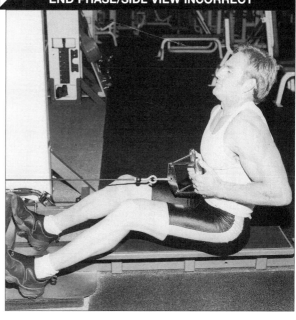

▶ **END PHASE/FRONT VIEW**

**key points**

KEEP THE CHEST UPLIFTED AND OPEN, INITIATING MOVEMENT FROM THE SHOULDER BLADES. SQUEEZE THE SHOULDER BLADES TOGETHER AT THE END PHASE.

**things to avoid**

AVOID USING THE ARM MUSCLES, WINGING OUT THE ELBOWS, AND COLLAPSING THE CHEST (THIS INHIBITS SHOULDER BLADE MOVEMENT). MAKE SURE THE ELBOWS ARE NOT PULLED TOO FAR BACK IN THE FINAL PHASE.

# one-arm dumbbell row

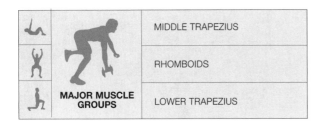

| | | MIDDLE TRAPEZIUS |
| --- | --- | --- |
| | | RHOMBOIDS |
| | **MAJOR MUSCLE GROUPS** | LOWER TRAPEZIUS |

**This is an advanced move requiring stabilization, core posture, and the ability to isolate specific muscle groups. It is extremely effective if done properly.**

**BEGINNING PHASE** ▶

### 1

Grasp the dumbbell with an even grip. Have the arm and knee on the side not being worked stabilized on the flat bench.

### 2

The leg on the floor (of the side being worked) should be slightly bent, so as to create a flat, tablelike back.

### 3

Start with the arm fully extended down. Avoid rotation of the back.

**key points**

KEEP THE CHEST UPLIFTED AND OPEN, INITIATING MOVEMENT FROM THE SHOULDER BLADE. RETRACT THE ENTIRE SHOULDER BLADE AS A SINGLE UNIT.

**things to avoid**

AVOID USING THE ARM MUSCLES, WINGING OUT THE ELBOW, AND COLLAPSING THE CHEST (THIS INHIBITS SHOULDER BLADE MOVEMENT). MAKE SURE THE ELBOW IS NOT PULLED TOO FAR UP IN THE FINAL PHASE. ALSO, AVOID ROTATING THE BACK DURING THE MOVEMENT.

| ▶ END PHASE ▶ | ▶ END PHASE INCORRECT |
| --- | --- |

4

Initiate movement by opening the chest cavity while pulling the entire shoulder blade in toward the spine. Continue the pull until the upper arm is horizontal. In the final position, the shoulder blade should be fully retracted (pulled in toward the spine) and the upper chest should be uplifted and open.

5

Do not lift the elbow past the level of the shoulder joint. The shoulder should not be rolled forward.

# the shoulder muscles

chapter seven

THINGS YOU WILL LEARN IN THIS CHAPTER:

**ARNOLDS**

**CYBEX® VR-2 OVERHEAD PRESS**

**PEC-DEC REVERSE FLY**

**DUMBBELL REVERSE FLY**

**CYBEX® VR-2 REVERSE FLY**

**CYBEX® VR-2 REVERSE BOX**

**DUMBBELL LATERAL RAISES**

**DUMBBELL ROTATORS**

# the shoulder muscles

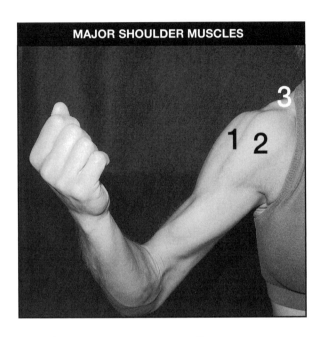

**MAJOR SHOULDER MUSCLES**

1
**MIDDLE DELTOID**

2
**ANTERIOR (FRONT) DELTOID**

3
**UPPER TRAPEZIUS (TRAPS)**

The shoulder muscles of many who work out are often overtrained and improperly isolated because the tendency is to let the upper traps dominate the movements.

To effectively isolate and train the shoulder muscles, it is essential to first learn to retract and anchor the shoulder blades. Once you can do this without compensating with your arms and upper traps or collapsing the sternum, you can isolate and train your shoulder muscles effectively. In addition, this anchoring capability helps to alleviate shoulder impingement syndrome, which is often a problem when working the shoulders.

The shoulder joint is the most mobile—and yet often the most unstable—joint in the body. To avoid imbalances and resultant problems, a proper BAM Superset combination is needed when training the shoulders. Several options are available, including the following:

1. Arnolds in combination with biceps alone or with both biceps and triceps (a nice three-exercise circuit)

2. Arnolds with an upper back pulldown exercise

3. Lateral raises with rotators

4. The Cybex overhead press with a reverse or rear deltoid fly exercise

It also is possible to superset any shoulder exercise with an upper back exercise. Examples of exercises to combine in BAM Supersets are in Chapter 11, "Designing Your Own Workout."

Eight effective shoulder exercises are shown next. Remember that when doing these exercises, it is important to maintain balance and not overtrain these muscles.

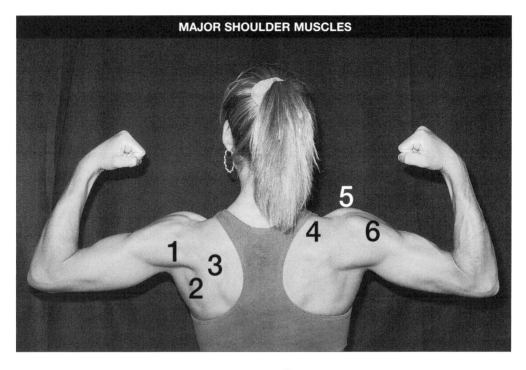

**MAJOR SHOULDER MUSCLES**

**1**
POSTERIOR (REAR)
DELTOID

**2**
TERES MINOR
(ROTATOR CUFF
MUSCLE)

**3**
INFRASPINATUS
(ROTATOR CUFF
MUSCLE)

**4**
UPPER TRAPEZIUS
(TRAPS)

**5**
ANTERIOR (FRONT)
DELTOID

**6**
MIDDLE DELTOID

# arnolds

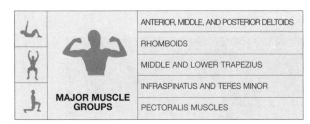

| | ANTERIOR, MIDDLE, AND POSTERIOR DELTOIDS |
|---|---|
| | RHOMBOIDS |
| | MIDDLE AND LOWER TRAPEZIUS |
| | INFRASPINATUS AND TERES MINOR |
| **MAJOR MUSCLE GROUPS** | PECTORALIS MUSCLES |

**This is a tremendous exercise for the shoulders and upper extremities. It requires the body to maintain core posture while utilizing a combination of muscle groups. It is also a great exercise to help in determining upper body imbalances. This is our personal favorite for the upper body.**

### BEGINNING PHASE/SIDE VIEW ▶

### MIDDLE PHASE/BACK VIEW ▶

## 1

Use a 90-degree angle bench for this exercise. Keep the back flat against the bench during the entire movement by pulling the abdominal muscles into the spine.

## 2

Begin with the arms bent at a 90-degree angle, the elbows together, the dumbbells at eye level, and the palms together, facing each other.

## 3

Rotate the arms back into a box/square position until they are in alignment with the ears (middle of body). At this point, the upper arms should be parallel to the ground. When moving from front to back, focus on moving the arms by using the shoulder blades (think of your arms as a double door, each hinging at the shoulder joint).

key points

**KEEP THE BACK FLAT AGAINST THE BACK PAD AND FOCUS ON MOVING THE ARMS FROM THE SHOULDER BLADES.**

things to avoid

**AVOID ARCHING THE BACK, COLLAPSING THE STERNUM, SHRUGGING THE SHOULDERS, AND OVERROTATING THE WRISTS AND ELBOWS.**

## MIDDLE PHASE/FRONT VIEW

4

Once the arms are square, make sure that the back is flat against the bench and the shoulders are anchored down and back (don't shrug). Press up half way without engaging the triceps.

Reverse the movement in a controlled motion to the starting position.

## END PHASE/FRONT VIEW

5

During the entire movement, the wrists, elbows, and shoulder joints should remain aligned and square.

# cybex® vr-2
## overhead press

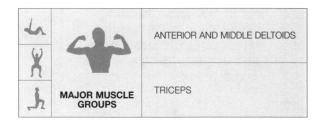

| | |
|---|---|
| | ANTERIOR AND MIDDLE DELTOIDS |
| **MAJOR MUSCLE GROUPS** | TRICEPS |

**This is a good power and strength exercise.**

| BEGINNING PHASE/FRONT VIEW ▶▶ | MIDDLE PHASE/SIDE VIEW INCORRECT ▶ |
|---|---|

### 1

Adjust the seat height so that the horizontal handles are in line with the lower ear.

### 2

Take an overhand grip on the outside handles. Keep the back flat against the bench by pulling in the abdominal muscles. This is very important as a foundation for the push. Press up in an arclike inward movement until the arms are fully extended overhead.

key points

**KEEP THE ELBOWS ALIGNED UNDER THE HANDLES AT ALL TIMES AND KEEP THE BACK FLAT AGAINST THE PAD.**

things to avoid

**AVOID ARCHING THE BACK, COLLAPSING THE STERNUM, SHRUGGING THE SHOULDERS, AND OVERROTATING THE WRISTS AND ELBOWS.**

▶ **END PHASE/FRONT VIEW**

3

During the entire movement, the wrists and elbows should be aligned directly under the handles. This helps to isolate the deltoids.

**NOTE**

It should be noted that this technique can be applied to any standard overhead shoulder press machine (minus the arclike inward movement).

# pec-dec
## reverse fly

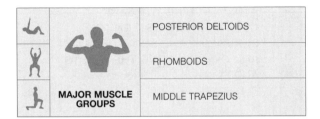

| | | POSTERIOR DELTOIDS |
|---|---|---|
| | | RHOMBOIDS |
| | **MAJOR MUSCLE GROUPS** | MIDDLE TRAPEZIUS |

**This is an effective posterior deltoid exercise when done properly.**

| BEGINNING PHASE/SIDE VIEW ▶ ▶ ▶ | END PHASE/SIDE VIEW ▶ |
|---|---|

**1**

Adjust the seat height so that the thumbs are even with the shoulders when gripping the handles.

**2**

Begin with the arms in a "V" shape position, making sure that the wrists, elbows, and shoulders are in line.

**3**

Move the arms back, hinging at the shoulder joints, maintaining the "V" shape position of the arms throughout the entire movement. At the end of the movement, the arms should be at midline (even with the ears) and forming a giant "W" when viewed from behind. The shoulders should be anchored, not shrugged.

MAINTAIN A "V" SHAPE WITH THE ARMS AND HINGE AT THE SHOULDER JOINT.

**END PHASE/BACK VIEW**

things to avoid

AVOID COLLAPSING THE STERNUM, SHRUGGING THE SHOULDERS, AND ROTATING THE ELBOWS BACK.

**END PHASE/SIDE VIEW INCORRECT**

**END PHASE/BACK VIEW INCORRECT**

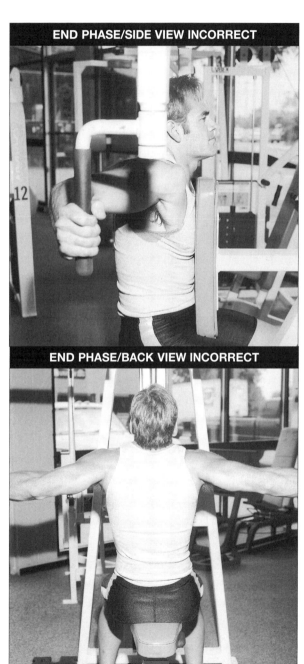

# dumbbell
## reverse fly

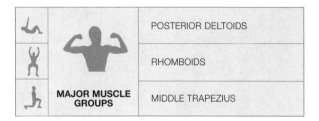

| | | |
|---|---|---|
| | **MAJOR MUSCLE GROUPS** | POSTERIOR DELTOIDS |
| | | RHOMBOIDS |
| | | MIDDLE TRAPEZIUS |

**This is an effective posterior deltoid exercise when done properly.**

**BEGINNING PHASE/SIDE VIEW** ▶

1

Use an inclined bench (30-degree angle) for this exercise. Straddle the bench, face down. Using an even grip on the dumbbells, start with the thumbs even with the shoulders. Begin with the arms in a "V" shape position, making sure that the wrists, elbows, and shoulders are in line.

**MAINTAIN A "V" SHAPE WITH THE ARMS AND HINGE AT THE SHOULDER JOINT.**

**AVOID COLLAPSING THE STERNUM, SHRUGGING THE SHOULDERS, AND ROTATING THE ELBOWS BACK.**

▶ **END PHASE/BACK VIEW**

2

Move the arms back, hinging at the shoulder joints, maintaining the "V" shape position of the arms throughout the entire movement. At the end of the movement, the arms should be at midline (even with the ears) and forming a giant "W" when viewed from behind. The shoulders should be anchored, not shrugged.

# cybex® vr-2
## reverse fly

| | | |
|---|---|---|
| 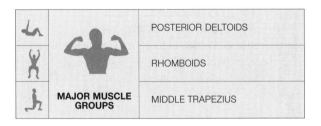 | **MAJOR MUSCLE GROUPS** | POSTERIOR DELTOIDS |
| | | RHOMBOIDS |
| | | MIDDLE TRAPEZIUS |

**This exercise targets the posterior deltoids. When done properly, it also strengthens the neck.**

| BEGINNING PHASE/SIDE VIEW ▶ ▶ ▶ | END PHASE/SIDE VIEW ▶ |
|---|---|

### 1

Adjust the seat height so that the chest pad is lined up with the middle/lower portion of your sternum. Grip the lower third of the vertical handles.

### 2

Begin with the arms in a "V" shape position, making sure that the wrists, elbows, and shoulders are in line.

**MAINTAIN A "V" SHAPE WITH THE ARMS AND HINGE AT THE SHOULDER JOINT.**

**AVOID COLLAPSING THE STERNUM, SHRUGGING THE SHOULDERS, FLEXING THE WRISTS, AND ROTATING THE ELBOWS BACK.**

▶ **END PHASE/BACK VIEW**

3

Move the arms back, hinging at the shoulder joints, maintaining the "V" shape position of the arms throughout the entire movement. At the end of the movement, the arms should be at midline (even with the ears) and forming a giant "W" when viewed from behind. The shoulders should be anchored, not shrugged.

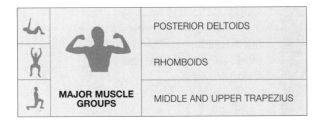

# cybex® vr-2
## reverse box

| | | |
|---|---|---|
| 🧍 | | POSTERIOR DELTOIDS |
| 🧍 | 💪 | RHOMBOIDS |
| 🧍 | **MAJOR MUSCLE GROUPS** | MIDDLE AND UPPER TRAPEZIUS |

**This is an intense exercise. It requires precise technique and, when done properly, will also help to strengthen the neck.**

| BEGINNING PHASE/SIDE VIEW ▶ ▶ ▶ | END PHASE/SIDE VIEW ▶ |
|---|---|

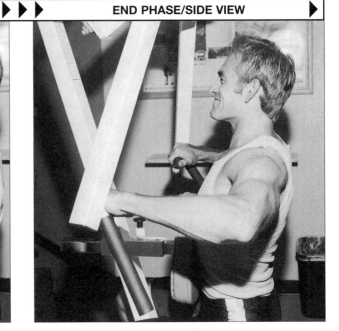

**1**

Adjust the seat height so that the chest pad is lined up with the middle/lower portion of your sternum. Take a wide grip on the horizontal handles.

**2**

Begin with the arms fully extended and the sternum/chest uplifted. Take the arms back to a right angle box position, keeping the elbows level to the ground.

**KEEP THE STERNUM UPLIFTED AND THE CHEST OPEN. SQUARE THE ARMS AT THE END PHASE.**

**AVOID COLLAPSING THE STERNUM, SHRUGGING THE SHOULDERS, AND ROTATING THE ELBOWS BACK.**

▶ **END PHASE/BACK VIEW**

3

Return in a controlled motion to the starting position.

# dumbbell lateral raises

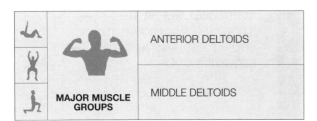

| | | |
|---|---|---|
|  | | ANTERIOR DELTOIDS |
| | **MAJOR MUSCLE GROUPS** | MIDDLE DELTOIDS |

**This exercise does not require much weight when performed with precise technique. It is great for developing width in the shoulders.**

| BEGINNING PHASE/FRONT VIEW ▶ ▶ ▶ | END PHASE/FRONT VIEW ▶ |
|---|---|

### 1

Using an even grip on the dumbbells, start with the hands in front of the legs and the arms slightly bent. It is important to maintain core posture throughout the entire movement, using a slight knee bend.

### 2

Move the arms up and diagonally back, hinging at the shoulder joints. Be sure to maintain the same position in the arms throughout the entire movement. At the end of the movement, the

**key points**

HINGE AT THE SHOULDER JOINT, NOT AT THE ELBOW JOINT, AND FINISH WITH THE DUMBBELLS ALIGNED WITH THE EARS.

**things to avoid**

AVOID COLLAPSING THE STERNUM, SHRUGGING THE SHOULDERS, ROTATING THE ELBOWS TOO FAR FORWARD OR BACKWARD, AND ROCKING AT THE WAIST OR HIPS.

▶ END PHASE/SIDE VIEW

▶▶ END PHASE/SIDE VIEW INCORRECT

dumbbells should be at midline (even with the ears) and slightly turned up. The shoulders should be anchored, not shrugged.

# dumbbell
## rotators

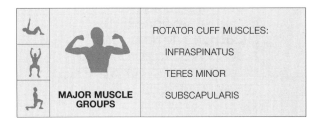

| | ROTATOR CUFF MUSCLES: |
| | INFRASPINATUS |
| | TERES MINOR |
| **MAJOR MUSCLE GROUPS** | SUBSCAPULARIS |

This is a great warm-up or cool-down exercise. It should be incorporated into a workout routine when shoulder problems exist.

**BEGINNING PHASE/SIDE VIEW** ▶

1

Using an even grip on the dumbbells, start with the arms bent at 90 degrees and the elbows fixed at your sides. It is important to maintain core posture throughout the entire movement, using a slight knee bend.

key points

MAINTAIN ARMS AT A
90-DEGREE ANGLE AND
KEEP THE ELBOWS FIXED.

things to avoid

AVOID MOVING THE ARMS ABOVE OR
BELOW 90 DEGREES, EXTENDING THE
WRISTS TO INCREASE THE RANGE,
SWINGING THE ELBOWS FORWARD OR
BACKWARD, COLLAPSING THE
STERNUM, SHRUGGING THE SHOULDERS,
AND ROCKING AT THE WAIST OR HIPS.

▶ END PHASE/FRONT VIEW

2

Rotate the lower arms from
the front of the body, hinging
at the elbow joint until even
with the midline of the body. It
is important to keep a
moderately quick pace in
order to isolate the rotator
cuff muscles; going too
slow results in tension
in the biceps.

THINGS YOU WILL LEARN IN THIS CHAPTER:

**TRICEP ROPE PULLDOWNS**

**DUMBBELL TRICEP KICKBACKS**

**DUMBBELL CURLS**

**HAMMER CURLS**

**CYBEX® ARM CURL MACHINE**

# the arm muscles

### 1
FOREARM FLEXORS

### 2
BICEPS

### 3
TRICEPS

The arm and chest muscles are the focus of most individuals' upper body training programs. This can lead to overtraining and significant upper body imbalances. To avoid these imbalances, we recommend that the biceps and triceps be trained together using the BAM Superset technique. This helps create symmetry in the arm muscles and provides a better workout "pump."

To effectively isolate and train the arm muscles, it is important to fix the elbow in one position, typically at the sides of the body, and to stabilize the shoulder joint. This isolates muscle action at the elbow joint, effectively targeting the biceps, brachialis, and triceps. A common

MAJOR ARM MUSCLES (FRONT)

mistake is to wing out or raise up the elbows. This hinders the isolation of the bicep and tricep muscles.

This chapter includes five effective arm exercises. It is important to use the BAM Superset technique and alternate between the bicep and tricep exercises. (See Chapter 11, "Designing Your Own Workout" for examples of exercises to combine in BAM Supersets.)

1

**BRACHIALIS**

2

**BRACHIORADIALIS**

3

**FOREARM EXTENSORS**

MAJOR ARM MUSCLES (BACK)

# tricep rope pulldowns

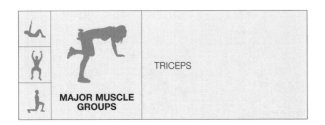

MAJOR MUSCLE GROUPS

TRICEPS

This is the best overall tricep exercise. When done properly, it does not place any strain on the shoulders (as opposed to overhead tricep movements).

| BEGINNING PHASE ▶ ▶ ▶ | END PHASE ▶ |
|---|---|

## 1
Begin with elbows at your sides and hands together at chest height. Maintain a core posture stance throughout the entire movement.

## 2
Pull the rope down. At belly height, start taking the hands out to the sides of the legs. At the bottom of the exercise, the arms should be fully extended and you should feel a full contraction (cramping) of the tricep muscles. Return in a controlled motion to the starting position.

**KEEP THE ELBOWS FIXED AT YOUR SIDES, HINGING ONLY AT THE ELBOW JOINT.**

**AVOID LEANING OVER THE ROPE AND COLLAPSING THE STERNUM. KEEP THE SHOULDERS FROM ROLLING FORWARD AND THE ELBOWS FROM WINGING OUT.**

▶ **END PHASE INCORRECT**

3

During the entire movement, the upper arms should remain absolutely fixed in a vertical position. The elbows should remain fixed at the sides of the body as well (do *not* wing elbows out). All movement should take place in the elbow joint, no other joints should be involved.

# dumbbell tricep kickbacks

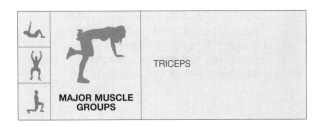

TRICEPS

**MAJOR MUSCLE GROUPS**

**This exercise requires precise technique to be effective.**

| BEGINNING PHASE | ▶▶ BEGINNING PHASE INCORRECT ▶ |
| --- | --- |

## 1
Grasp the dumbbell with an even grip. Have the arm and knee on the side not being worked stabilized on the flat bench.

## 2
The leg on the floor should be slightly bent so as to create a flat, tablelike back.

key points

**KEEP THE UPPER ARM LEVEL WITH THE GROUND, HINGING ONLY AT THE ELBOW JOINT.**

things to avoid

**AVOID ROLLING THE SHOULDER FORWARD, WINGING OUT THE ELBOW, AND MOVING MORE THAN JUST THE LOWER ARM TO PERFORM THE EXERCISE.**

| END PHASE | END PHASE INCORRECT |
|---|---|

3

4

Start with the upper arm horizontal and level with the upper back. The lower arm should be vertical (straight down). The elbow should remain fixed at the side of the body during the entire exercise.

"Kickback" the lower arm, hinging at the elbow joint until it is aligned with the upper arm. At the end phase, the entire arm should be horizontal and level with the back.

# dumbbell
## curls

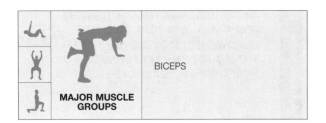

BICEPS

**MAJOR MUSCLE GROUPS**

**This is a great bicep development exercise. When done with proper technique, it is also effective for anterior shoulder stabilization.**

BEGINNING PHASE ▶

1

### NOTE

This exercise can be performed by alternating one arm at a time or using both arms at the same time in a seated or standing position.

This exercise can also be done with a straight bar, or "easy curl" bar (with or without weights added).

Take an even grip on the dumbbells. Begin with elbows at your sides and arms fully extended along the sides of the legs. Hands should be completely supinated (palms turned up) during the entire movement. Maintain a core posture stance throughout the entire movement.

**KEEP THE ELBOWS FIXED AT YOUR SIDES AND THE HANDS SUPINATED (PALMS TURNED UP) AT ALL TIMES.**

**AVOID ROCKING THE BODY AND MOVING THE ELBOWS AWAY FROM THE SIDES OF THE BODY.**

▶ **END PHASE**

2     3

Curl up the dumbbells until they are level with the shoulders. Weights and hands should be in a straight line. Return in a controlled motion to the starting position.

During the entire movement, the upper arms should remain absolutely fixed in a vertical position. The elbows should remain fixed at the sides of the body as well (do not wing elbows out or move them forward). All movement should take place in the elbow joint; no other joints should be involved.

# hammer
## curls

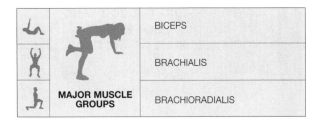

| | | |
|---|---|---|
| | | BICEPS |
| | | BRACHIALIS |
| | **MAJOR MUSCLE GROUPS** | BRACHIORADIALIS |

**This is a good power and strength exercise for the arms that isolates the brachialis muscles. It is great for developing width in your arms.**

**BEGINNING PHASE** ▶

### 1

Take an even grip on the dumbbells. Begin with elbows at your sides and arms fully extended along the sides of the legs. Hands should be in a neutral position with thumbs forward during the entire movement. Maintain a core posture stance throughout the entire movement.

### 2

Curl up the dumbbells until they are level with the shoulders. Return in a controlled motion to the starting position.

key points

KEEP THE ELBOWS FIXED AT
YOUR SIDES AND KEEP A
NEUTRAL HAND GRIP WITH
THUMBS UP AT ALL TIMES.

things to avoid

AVOID ROCKING THE BODY AND
MOVING THE ELBOWS AWAY
FROM THE SIDES OF THE BODY.

▶ END PHASE

3

During the entire movement,
the upper arms should remain
absolutely fixed in a vertical
position. The elbows should
remain fixed at the sides of
the body as well (do not wing
elbows out or move them

forward). All movement
should take place in the
elbow joint; no other joints
should be involved.

**NOTE**

This exercise can be
performed by alternating one
arm at a time or using both
arms at the same time.

# cybex® arm curl machine

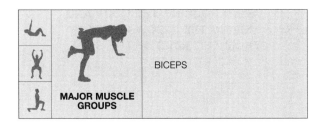

| | | |
|---|---|---|
| | | BICEPS |
| | **MAJOR MUSCLE GROUPS** | |

**This is an alternative bicep exercise that may be preferred if you have lower back problems.**

**BEGINNING PHASE** ▶

## 1

Take an even grip on the handles. Begin with the elbows in line with the shoulders. Hands should be completely supinated (palms turned up) during the entire movement. Maintain an uplifted sternum and anchored shoulder blades throughout the entire movement.

**key points**

**KEEP THE STERNUM UPLIFTED, THE SHOULDERS ANCHORED, AND THE WRISTS, ELBOWS, AND SHOULDERS IN LINE.**

**things to avoid**

**AVOID ROCKING THE BODY AND MOVING THE ELBOWS LATERALLY.**

▶ **END PHASE**

**2**

Curl up until the forearms are vertical. Return in a controlled motion to the starting position.

**3**

The upper arms and elbows should remain absolutely fixed during the entire movement. All movement should take place in the elbow joint; no other joints should be involved.

THINGS YOU WILL LEARN IN THIS CHAPTER:

# the leg muscles

There are many variables to consider when training the lower body. Lower back, hip, and knee problems are commonplace, creating asymmetry and imbalances in the lower extremities. These imbalances are compounded by the fact that most people working out in a health club or gym do not effectively stabilize their core muscles when training the lower body. Compensatory movement patterns often result, which can lead to increased imbalances and weaknesses in the body.

To avoid this, we recommend building a solid base of core musculature before doing any heavy lifting or complex movements in training the lower body. To establish this solid base, first identify weaknesses that may exist in the lower body and core musculature. (See Chapter 3, "Posture and Ergonomics," and Chapter 10, "The Abdominal and Lower Back Muscles," for more information.) We recommend starting with hip abduction and adduction along with the seated leg curl machine (use the prone leg curl machine if the seated leg curl machine is not available) for the first one to two weeks before moving on to more complex movements.

Once a base has been established, BAM Superset combinations involving major muscle groups in the legs should be incorporated into the workout. It is important to maintain balance between the quadriceps and hamstring muscles, as well as between the abducting and adducting muscles, and the hip flexor and extensor muscle groups. To maintain balance in the core musculature, integrate the training of the abdominal and lower torso muscles into the leg workout.

This chapter includes 14 effective leg exercises that should be combined in BAM Supersets. The exercises presented in Chapter 10, "The Abdominal and Lower Back Muscles," can also be integrated into the leg muscle BAM Supersets. (Examples of exercises to combine in BAM Supersets are in Chapter 11, "Designing Your Own Workout.")

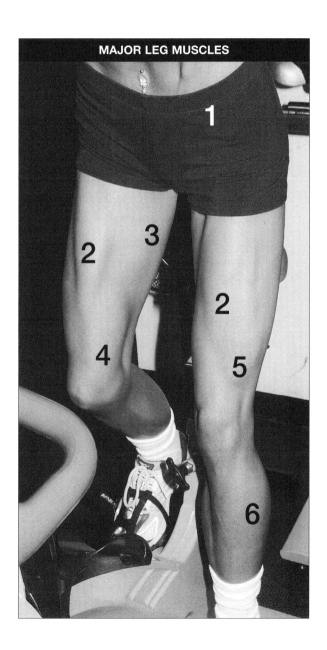

**MAJOR LEG MUSCLES**

1

**PSOAS
(HIP FLEXORS)**

2

**QUADRICEPS
(QUADS)**

3

**ADDUCTORS**

4

**VASTUS MEDIALIS
(LOWER INSERTION)**

5

**VASTUS LATERALIS
(LOWER INSERTION)**

6

**TIBIALIS ANTERIOR**

7

**TENSOR FASCIA LATAE AND ILIOTIBIAL (IT) BAND (ABDUCTORS)**

8

**HAMSTRINGS**

9

**GASTROCNEMIUS (CALVES)**

10

**SOLEUS**

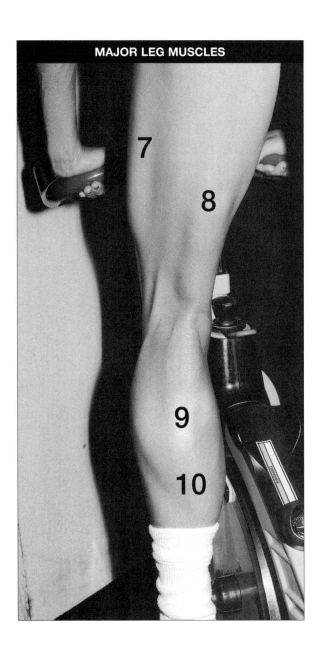

MAJOR LEG MUSCLES

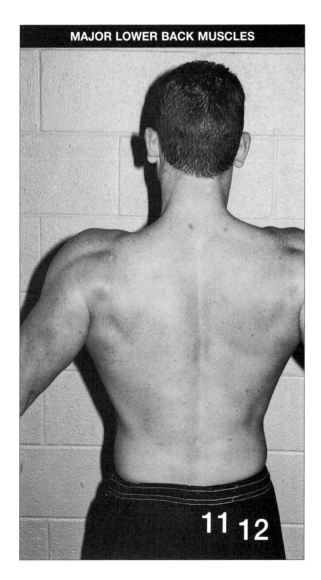

**MAJOR LOWER BACK MUSCLES**

**11**

**GLUTEAL MUSCLES
(GLUTES)**

**12**

**PIRIFORMIS**

# cybex® seated leg curls

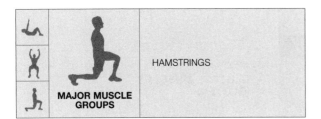

HAMSTRINGS

**MAJOR MUSCLE
GROUPS**

**This is a great hamstring exercise. It is very important to utilize correct back, leg pad, and range settings (limit range, if necessary).**

| BEGINNING PHASE ▶▶ | BEGINNING PHASE INCORRECT ▶ |
|---|---|

## 1

Adjust the seat back and leg bar to their proper position. Align the knees with the machine's axis of rotation, keeping the back flat on the pad. The top leg pad brace should fit snugly on top of the thighs.

## 2

Curl legs down in a slow, controlled movement, making sure that you achieve full contraction at the bottom phase of the movement. It is helpful to imagine that you are moving your heels to your glutes to achieve a maximum contraction of the hamstrings. In addition, the feet should be flexed (toes pointed back toward the chest) at the top of the motion.

**MAINTAIN SLOW AND CONTROLLED MOVEMENT, PERFORMING AS FULL A RANGE OF MOTION AS POSSIBLE WHILE KEEPING THE BACK FLAT.**

things to avoid

**AVOID PULLING THE BACK AND HIPS AWAY FROM THE BACK PAD OR ARCHING THE BACK AS YOU COMPLETE THE CURL. IF YOU CANNOT MAINTAIN A FLAT BACK DURING THE ENTIRE RANGE OF THE MOVEMENT YOU MAY BE USING TOO MUCH WEIGHT.**

▶ END PHASE

▶▶ END PHASE INCORRECT

3

The return motion should be slow and controlled as well, bringing the knees to a full extension. If you have knee problems, it might be best to limit the range of motion by using the range limiting pins; a suggested setting would be 3 and 13.

**NOTE**

This exercise can be performed one leg at a time. The leg not being worked remains up until the other leg completes a full repetition (beginning phase to end phase and back to beginning phase).

# prone leg curls

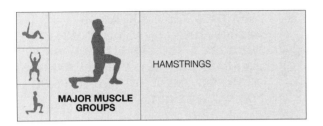

HAMSTRINGS

**MAJOR MUSCLE
GROUPS**

**This is a good hamstring exercise. However, the seated
leg curl would be preferred if lower back problems exist.**

| BEGINNING PHASE ▶ ▶ ▶ | END PHASE ▶ |
|---|---|

## 1

Adjust the leg bar so that
when you are in position on
the machine the hips are over
the center ridge and the leg
pad is 1 or 2 inches above
the ankle joint.

## 2

Curl the legs up in a slow,
controlled movement, making
sure that you achieve full
contraction at the top phase
of the movement. It is helpful
to imagine that you are
moving your heels to your
glutes to achieve a maximum
contraction of the hamstrings.

**MAINTAIN SLOW AND CONTROLLED MOVEMENT, PERFORMING AS FULL A RANGE OF MOTION AS POSSIBLE WHILE KEEPING THE HIPS DOWN.**

**AVOID LIFTING THE HIPS OFF OF THE PAD. IF YOU CANNOT MAINTAIN A FLAT PELVIS DURING THE ENTIRE RANGE OF THE MOVEMENT, YOU MAY BE USING TOO MUCH WEIGHT.**

**MIDDLE PHASE INCORRECT**

3

The return motion should be slow and controlled as well, bringing the knees to a full extension.

# cybex® hip abduction

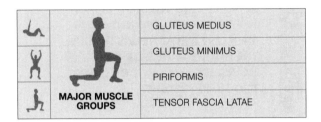

| | | GLUTEUS MEDIUS |
|---|---|---|
| | | GLUTEUS MINIMUS |
| | | PIRIFORMIS |
| | **MAJOR MUSCLE GROUPS** | TENSOR FASCIA LATAE |

**This is a key beginner exercise that is important in core and pelvic stabilization.**

**BEGINNING PHASE** ▶

## 1

Place feet on the appropriate foot rung, so that upper and lower legs are at right angles. Generally, individuals over 6 feet in height will be on the lower rung and those under 6 feet will be on the upper rung.

## 2

Begin with good core posture, the abs engaged, and the back flat against the pad. Initiate movement from the hip socket, trying to use the hip muscles to perform the movement (don't initiate the push with knees against

**INITIATE MOVEMENT FROM THE HIP SOCKET AND USE BOTH LEGS EVENLY.**

**AVOID USING ONE LEG MORE THAN THE OTHER. ALSO AVOID ARCHING THE BACK OR MOVING THE HIPS AWAY FROM THE BACK PAD.**

▶ **END PHASE**

3

the pads). Move the legs out evenly, achieving as great a range of motion as possible, without compromising your technique.

The return motion should be slow and controlled as well, bringing the legs back to center.

# cybex® hip adduction

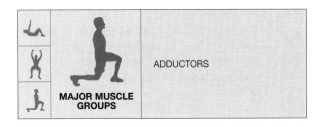

| MAJOR MUSCLE GROUPS | ADDUCTORS |
|---|---|

**This is a key beginner exercise important in core and pelvic stabilization.**

**BEGINNING PHASE** ▶

## 1

Place feet on the appropriate foot rung, so that upper and lower legs are at right angles. Generally, individuals over 6 feet in height will be on the lower rung and those under 6 feet will be on the upper rung.

## 2

Begin with good core posture, the abs engaged, and the back flat against the pad with the leg supports positioned out as wide as comfortably possible. Initiate movement from the upper adductors (groin). Bring legs

**key points**

**INITIATE MOVEMENT FROM THE UPPER ADDUCTORS AND USE BOTH LEGS EVENLY.**

**things to avoid**

**AVOID USING ONE LEG MORE THAN THE OTHER. ALSO AVOID ARCHING THE BACK OR MOVING THE HIPS AWAY FROM THE BACK PAD.**

▶ **END PHASE**

3

into the center using both legs equally until the leg pads meet.

The return motion should be slow and controlled.

# standing cable hip abduction

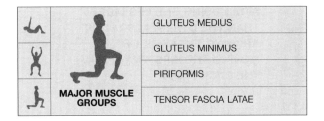

| | | |
|---|---|---|
| | | GLUTEUS MEDIUS |
| | | GLUTEUS MINIMUS |
| | | PIRIFORMIS |
| | **MAJOR MUSCLE GROUPS** | TENSOR FASCIA LATAE |

**This exercise is important in core and pelvic stabilization.**

**BEGINNING PHASE** ▶

### 1

Put the strap on the outside ankle. Stabilize the body by holding on to the cable machine handle.

### 2

Begin with good core posture, the abs engaged, and the hips square. Keeping the leg straight, initiate movement from the hip socket, focusing on the outer glute and hip muscles to

**INITIATE MOVEMENT FROM THE HIP SOCKET, KEEPING THE LEG STRAIGHT AT ALL TIMES.**

**AVOID QUICK AND FORCED MOVEMENT AND ROTATION OF THE HIPS AND BODY.**

▶ **END PHASE**

3

move the leg away from the center of the body. It is important not to rotate the body or the hips throughout the entire range of motion.

The return motion should be slow and controlled as well, bringing the leg back until even with the other foot.

# standing cable hip adduction

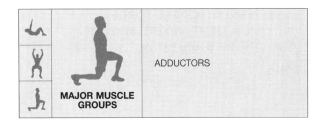

| | ADDUCTORS |
|---|---|
| **MAJOR MUSCLE GROUPS** | |

**This exercise is important in core and pelvic stabilization.**

BEGINNING PHASE ▶

### 1

Put the strap on the inside ankle. Stabilize the body by holding on to the cable machine handle.

### 2

Begin with a wide foot stance and good core posture, the abs engaged, and the hips square. Keeping the leg straight, initiate movement from the inner thigh, moving the leg across and in front of

**key points**

INITIATE MOVEMENT FROM THE INNER THIGH (ADDUCTORS), KEEPING THE LEG STRAIGHT AT ALL TIMES. AVOID EXCESSIVE ROTATION OF THE BODY.

**things to avoid**

AVOID QUICK AND FORCED MOVEMENT AND ROTATION OF THE HIPS AND BODY.

▶ END PHASE

3

the outside leg. During the movement, place your body weight on the outside leg. It is important not to rotate the body or the hips throughout the entire range of motion.

The return motion should be slow and controlled as well, bringing the leg back to the starting position.

# cybex®
# leg extensions

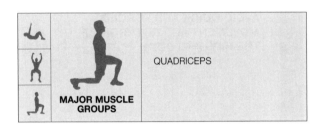

QUADRICEPS

**MAJOR MUSCLE GROUPS**

**This is a tremendous exercise for isolating the quadricep muscles. However, caution should be taken if knee problems exist.**

**BEGINNING PHASE** ▶

## 1

Adjust the seat back and leg bar to the proper position. Align the knee with the machine's axis of rotation, keeping the back flat on the pad.

## 2

Extend legs up in a slow, controlled movement, making sure you achieve full extension at the top phase of the movement. It is helpful to do an isometric contraction at the top for a second or a second and a half to help eliminate momentum from the movement. In addition, the feet should be flexed (toes pointed back toward the chest) at the top of the motion.

key points

**MAINTAIN SLOW AND CONTROLLED MOVEMENT, REMEMBERING TO SQUEEZE ISOMETRICALLY AT THE TOP OF THE MOTION.**

things to avoid

**AVOID GOING TOO FAST, SWINGING THE LEGS, AND USING THAT MOMENTUM TO ACCOMPLISH THE LIFT.**

▶ **END PHASE**

3

The return motion should be slow and controlled as well, bringing the knees to a right angle and not below (do *not* put the weight stack down). If you have knee problems, it might be best to limit the range of motion by only coming down half way but still coming up to a full extension.

**NOTE**

This exercise can be performed one leg at a time. The leg not being worked remains down until the other leg completes a full repetition (beginning phase to end phase and back to beginning phase).

# cybex® seated leg press

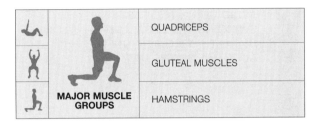

| | | |
|---|---|---|
| | | QUADRICEPS |
| | **MAJOR MUSCLE GROUPS** | GLUTEAL MUSCLES |
| | | HAMSTRINGS |

**This is a great beginning power and strength exercise.**

| BEGINNING PHASE | ▶ ▶ | BEGINNING PHASE INCORRECT |
|---|---|---|

### 1
Adjust the seat back and leg plate to the proper position so that the knees are at an angle slightly greater than 90 degrees and the lower back and sacrum are flat against the back pad.

### 2
Position the feet shoulder width apart with the toes at the level of the shoulders. Keep your foot centers aligned vertically.

### 3
Push in a controlled movement until the legs are just shy of full extension. (It is important not to hyperextend the knees in this movement.) Make sure to push equally on all three foot centers on both feet. The ankle, knee, and hip joints should remain aligned throughout the entire movement. Avoid the tendency to rotate the knees either inward or outward.

**key points**

PUSH EQUALLY ON BOTH FEET
WHILE MAINTAINING PROPER
KNEE AND HIP ALIGNMENT. KEEP
THE HIPS, LOWER BACK, AND
SACRUM FLAT AGAINST THE
BACK PAD.

**things to avoid**

AVOID LETTING THE SACRUM
CURL UP OFF OF THE BACK PAD.

### END PHASE

4

The return motion should be
controlled as well, bringing
the knees to a right angle or
slightly beyond, making sure
that the sacrum and lower
back do not lift away from
the back pad.

# plate-loaded leg press

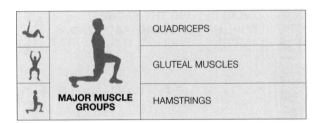

| | | QUADRICEPS |
| --- | --- | --- |
| | | GLUTEAL MUSCLES |
| | **MAJOR MUSCLE GROUPS** | HAMSTRINGS |

**This is an effective power and strength exercise.**

**BOTTOM PHASE/SIDE VIEW** ▶ ▶ **BOTTOM PHASE/SIDE VIEW INCORRECT** ▶

### 1

In the beginning position, the lower back and sacrum should be flat against the back pad.

### 2

Position the feet shoulder-width apart on the top third of the leg plate. Keep your foot centers aligned vertically.

### 3

Push weight off of the safety catches and release the catches. Push in a controlled movement until the legs are just shy of full extension. (It is important not to hyperextend the knees in this movement.) Make sure to push equally on all three foot centers on both feet. The ankle, knee, and hip joints should remain aligned throughout the entire movement.

### 4

The return motion should be controlled as well, bringing the knees to a right angle or slightly beyond, making sure that the sacrum and lower back do not lift away from the back pad.

## TOP PHASE/TOP VIEW

**key points**

PUSH EQUALLY ON BOTH FEET WHILE MAINTAINING PROPER KNEE AND HIP ALIGNMENT. KEEP THE HIPS, LOWER BACK, AND SACRUM FLAT AGAINST THE BACK PAD.

**things to avoid**

AVOID THE TENDENCY TO ROTATE THE KNEES EITHER INWARD OR OUTWARD. AVOID LETTING THE SACRUM CURL UP OFF OF THE BACK PAD.

### PROPER FOOT, KNEE, AND HIP ALIGNMENT ▶

### ▶ INCORRECT FOOT, KNEE, AND HIP ALIGNMENT

# butt blaster®

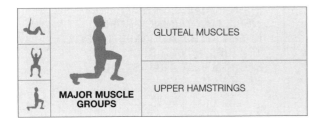

| | | |
|---|---|---|
| | **MAJOR MUSCLE GROUPS** | GLUTEAL MUSCLES |
| | | UPPER HAMSTRINGS |

**This is an effective exercise to isolate the glutes and upper hamstrings. Core stability is critical in performing this exercise properly.**

| BEGINNING PHASE/SIDE VIEW ▶▶▶ | END PHASE/SIDE VIEW ▶ |
|---|---|

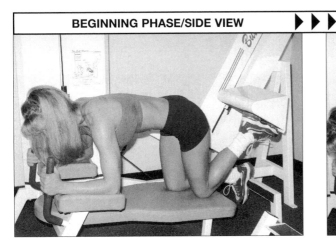

**1**

Begin with forearms on the arm pads and the nonworking leg supported on the foot bar. The working foot should be on the outer third of the push plate and squarely centered in the up and down plane. The back and hips should be level and flat like a table.

**2**

Push in a controlled movement until the leg is fully extended and you feel a distinct contraction in the upper hamstrings and glutes. It is very important to move the leg in a straight line, avoiding the tendency to shift the leg out.

**END PHASE/FRONT VIEW**

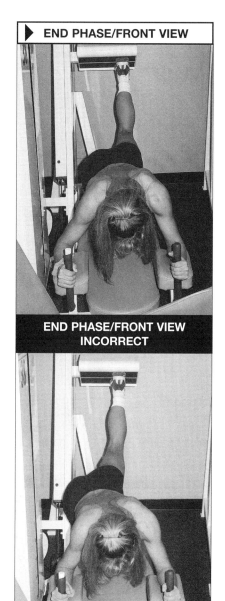

**END PHASE/FRONT VIEW**
**INCORRECT**

**KEEP THE HIPS AND BACK FLAT AND DON'T SHIFT WEIGHT TO THE NONWORKING HIP. MOVE THE WORKING LEG IN A STRAIGHT LINE AT ALL TIMES.**

**AVOID THE COMMON TENDENCY WHEN FATIGUED TO SHIFT YOUR BODY POSITION TOWARD THE NONWORKING HIP AND SKEW THE WORKING LEG OUTWARD. IT IS IMPORTANT TO MAINTAIN CORE MUSCLE INTEGRITY DURING THE ENTIRE MOVEMENT.**

# cybex®
## rotary calf

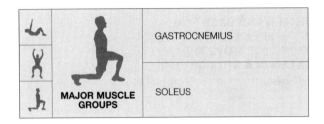

| | | GASTROCNEMIUS |
|---|---|---|
| | **MAJOR MUSCLE GROUPS** | SOLEUS |

**This is an effective calf exercise that limits stress on the lower back. We recommend a higher number of repetitions with reduced rest time between sets for this exercise.**

**BEGINNING PHASE** ▶

### 1

Adjust the seat setting so that the ankle joint is lined up with the axis of rotation of the machine. The balls of the feet should be evenly placed at shoulder width. The toes should be even with the top of the foot pad.

key points

**MAINTAIN A CONSTANT, SLIGHTLY BENT KNEE POSITION AND ISOLATE THE MOVEMENT TO THE HINGING OF THE ANKLE JOINT. PERFORM AS FULL A RANGE OF MOTION AS POSSIBLE IN A FLEXION AND EXTENSION MOVEMENT PATTERN.**

things to avoid

**AVOID THE COMMON TENDENCY TO INVOLVE THE KNEE JOINT AND RECRUIT THE QUADRICEP MUSCLES.**

▶ **END PHASE**

2

Knees should remain slightly bent during the entire movement. Hinging at the ankle, the feet should move through as full a range of motion as possible in a flexion/extension movement pattern.

**NOTE**

The calves are primarily composed of slow twitch (endurance) muscle fibers. Therefore, you should consider doing higher repetitions (15 to 20) with a shorter rest cycle between sets (20 to 25 seconds).

# swiss ball
## squats

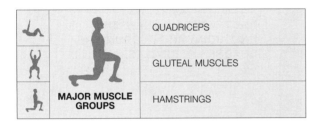

| | | QUADRICEPS |
|---|---|---|
| | | GLUTEAL MUSCLES |
| | **MAJOR MUSCLE GROUPS** | HAMSTRINGS |

**This is a good exercise to learn the squat. It can also be used with varying repetition speed and a pause/hold at the bottom phase to increase exercise intensity.**

| BEGINNING PHASE ▶ | END PHASE ▶ |
|---|---|

## 1
Position the ball at the height of the lower back and sacrum.

## 2
Position the feet shoulder-width apart with your foot centers aligned straight ahead. Your feet should be placed so that at the end phase (bottom) of the squat the knees form a 90-degree angle.

## 3
The upper body should be maintained in core posture throughout the entire exercise.

**PUSH EQUALLY ON BOTH FEET WHILE MAINTAINING PROPER KNEE AND HIP ALIGNMENT. KEEP THE STERNUM UP AND WRAP THE LOWER BACK AND SACRUM UNDER THE BALL.**

**AVOID THE TENDENCY TO ROTATE THE KNEES INWARD OR OUTWARD.**

**INCORRECT STERNUM COLLAPSE**

**INCORRECT LEAN**

**INCORRECT BALL TOO HIGH**

4

To begin, descend until the legs are at right angles. The sternum should be uplifted and the hips should wrap slightly underneath and around the ball. It is important to use the ball as a reference, not as a crutch. (Don't lean back on the ball as in the fourth picture.) Ascend in a controlled movement until knees are just short of full extension. Make sure to push equally on all three foot centers on both feet. The ankle, knee, and hip joints should remain aligned throughout the entire movement.

# smith machine
## squats

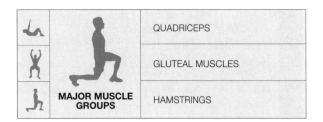

| | | QUADRICEPS |
|---|---|---|
| | | GLUTEAL MUSCLES |
| **MAJOR MUSCLE GROUPS** | | HAMSTRINGS |

**This is a good power and strength move.**

| TOP PHASE/FRONT VIEW ▶ | BOTTOM PHASE/FRONT VIEW ▶ |
|---|---|

**1**

Position the bar across the tops of the shoulder blades (upper back).

**2**

Position the feet shoulder-width apart with the foot centers aligned straight ahead or slightly turned out.

**3**

The upper body should be maintained in core posture throughout the entire exercise.

**4**

To begin, descend until legs are at right angles. The sternum should be uplifted with the hips underneath the weight of the bar and upper body.

**key points**

PUSH EQUALLY ON BOTH FEET WHILE MAINTAINING PROPER KNEE AND HIP ALIGNMENT. KEEP THE STERNUM UPLIFTED AND THE HIPS ALIGNED UNDER THE WEIGHT OF THE BAR AND THE UPPER BODY.

**things to avoid**

AVOID THE TENDENCY TO ROTATE THE KNEES INWARD OR OUTWARD. AVOID COLLAPSING THE STERNUM OR BENDING FORWARD AT THE WAIST.

▶ **BOTTOM PHASE/SIDE VIEW**

5

Ascend in a controlled movement until knees are just short of full extension. Be sure to push equally on all three foot centers on both feet. The ankle, knee, and hip joints should remain aligned throughout the entire movement.

# dumbbell lunges

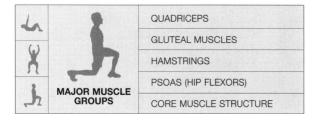

| | | |
|---|---|---|
| | **MAJOR MUSCLE GROUPS** | QUADRICEPS |
| | | GLUTEAL MUSCLES |
| | | HAMSTRINGS |
| | | PSOAS (HIP FLEXORS) |
| | | CORE MUSCLE STRUCTURE |

**This is a great exercise for the core musculature and for correcting pelvic and lower back imbalances. This exercise is our personal favorite for the lower body.**

| TOP PHASE ▶ | ▶ TOP PHASE/INCORRECT ▶ |
|---|---|

### 1
With dumbbells in hands, position the feet instep to instep 6 to 8 inches apart.

### 2
Step one foot forward about one and a half foot lengths. Step back with the other foot far enough to achieve a proper knee bend. The back heel should be elevated.

### 3
Align both feet toe to heel, facing straight ahead. Hips and shoulders should be square.

KEEP THE BACK KNEE ALIGNED UNDER THE HIP AND UPPER BODY. KEEP THE HIPS AND SHOULDERS SQUARE DURING THE ENTIRE MOVEMENT. EVENLY DISTRIBUTE BODY WEIGHT TO BOTH LEGS.

AVOID TORQUE AND ROTATION OF THE HIPS AND SHOULDERS (AS IN THE SECOND PICTURE, PAGE 148).

| ▶ BOTTOM PHASE | ▶ ▶ BOTTOM PHASE/INCORRECT |
|---|---|

**4**

Initiate the descent by immediately bending the back knee, bringing it directly under the hips. Continue the descent until both knees are at 90 degrees.

**5**

At the bottom position, it is important that the front knee is directly above the ankle.

things to avoid

AVOID PUTTING THE MAJORITY OF YOUR WEIGHT ON THE FRONT LEG (AS IN THE FOURTH PICTURE, PAGE 149).

AVOID ARCHING THE LOWER BACK (AS IN THE FIFTH PICTURE, PAGE 150).

BOTTOM PHASE/INCORRECT

## 6

In the bottom position, maintain core posture in the upper body and hips with no torque or rotation. The back knee, hip, and upper body should all be aligned.

## 7

To ascend, push back off of the front heel while pushing forward off of the back foot, trying to maintain equal weight distribution between both legs.

| BOTTOM PHASE/BACK VIEW | BOTTOM PHASE/BACK VIEW INCORRECT |
|---|---|
|  |  |

8

Do an equal number of
repetitions on both sides.

# the abdominal and lower back muscles

THINGS YOU WILL LEARN IN THIS CHAPTER:

**LOWER AB ROLL UPS ON THE
ABDOMINAL BENCH**

**LOWER AB ROLL UPS OFF THE FLOOR**

**UPPER AB ROLL UPS ON THE
ABDOMINAL BENCH**

**UPPER AB ROLL UPS OFF THE FLOOR**

**CYBEX® ROTARY TORSO**

**CYBEX® 45-DEGREE ANGLE
HYPEREXTENSIONS**

# the abdominal and lower back muscles

The abdominal and lower back muscles are major components of the core musculature that play an integral part in postural and lower body training. The common mistake made in training the abdominal muscles is primarily training the rectus abdominis and hip flexor muscles while not effectively targeting the obliques and transversus abdominis (the deepest muscular layer in the abdomen). By learning to train and effectively target the oblique and transversus abdominis muscles, you will develop a stronger core, help protect your lower back, and reduce your waistline.

Breathing is a key component in isolating and enhancing the contraction of the abdominal muscles. Since the abdominals are used in forced expiration, force air out through the mouth when initiating the contraction phase of an abdominal exercise. To further enhance the contraction and isolation of the deeper layer of abdominal wall musculature, try to hollow out (make concave) the belly by pulling the navel in toward the spine.

In training the lower back muscles, be careful not to overextend or overflex. We also recommend ending any

BAM Superset combination involving the lower back muscles with the abdominal component of that superset. This will help to reduce any lower back hypertonicity.

This chapter includes six effective exercises for the abdominal and lower back region that can be combined in BAM Supersets. These should be integrated with the exercises presented in Chapter 9, "The Leg Muscles." (Examples of exercises to combine in BAM Supersets are in Chapter 11, "Designing Your Own Workout.")

1

**OBLIQUES**

2

**UPPER ABDOMINALS**

3

**LOWER ABDOMINALS**

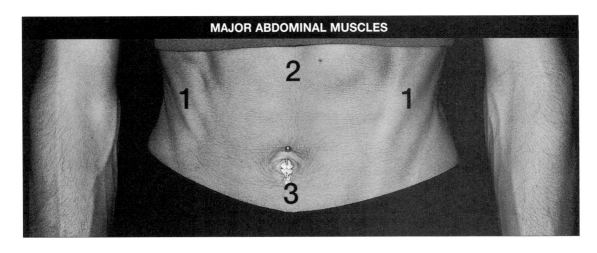

MAJOR ABDOMINAL MUSCLES

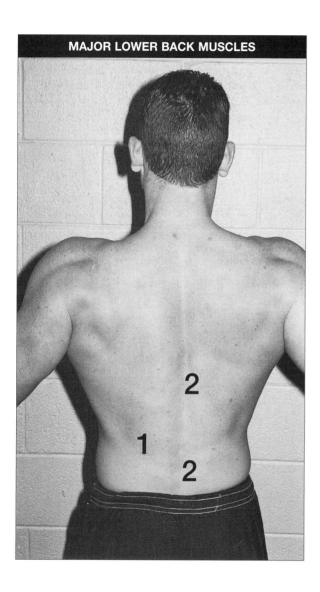

**MAJOR LOWER BACK MUSCLES**

1

**QUADRATUS
LUMBORUM**

2

**ERECTOR SPINAE**

# lower ab roll ups on the abdominal bench

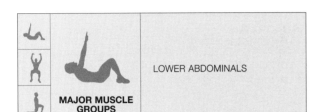

| MAJOR MUSCLE GROUPS | LOWER ABDOMINALS |

**This is an important exercise for lower back problems and core stabilization. It is a very effective abdominal strengthening exercise.**

| BEGINNING PHASE ▶▶ | BEGINNING PHASE INCORRECT ▶ |

## 1

Adjust the bench to the horizontal position (for a more advanced exercise, you can decline the angle of the bench). Stabilize the upper body by holding on to the handle. Do not use this hold to help pull your legs up.

## 2

With the back and sacrum flat on the bench, begin with the legs together and slightly bent at the 10 o'clock position (see the first picture). If you have weak lower abs or lower back problems, you might want to start with the knees bent at 90 degrees.

things to avoid

AVOID GOING TOO FAST, SWINGING THE LEGS, AND USING THAT MOMENTUM TO ACCOMPLISH THE MOVEMENT. ALSO, AVOID AN EXCESSIVE RANGE OF MOVEMENT WITH THE LEGS. DON'T EXTEND THE LEGS DOWN TOO FAR AS THIS PUTS A STRAIN ON THE LOWER BACK (SEE THE SECOND PICTURE),

AND DON'T CURL THE LEGS UP TOO FAR AS THIS DECREASES THE ISOLATION IN THE ABS AND SHIFTS THE EFFORT TO THE HIP FLEXORS, GREATLY REDUCING THE EFFECTIVENESS OF THE EXERCISE (SEE THE FOURTH PICTURE).

▶ END PHASE

▶▶ END PHASE INCORRECT

### 3

Initiate the movement by curling up the hips and then the lower back, lifting the lower back off of the bench. In the end phase the legs should be straight up and you should visualize your feet being pushed straight up toward the ceiling.

### 4

The return motion should be slow and controlled, visualizing the lower back rolling down one vertebra at a time until the sacrum is again flat on the bench and the legs are back at the 10 o'clock position.

key points

FOCUS ON CURLING UP THE HIPS AND LOWER BACK BY USING THE LOWER ABS. DO NOT USE THE MOMENTUM OF THE LEGS TO ACCOMPLISH THIS EXERCISE.

# lower ab roll ups
## off the floor

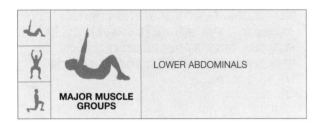

LOWER ABDOMINALS

**MAJOR MUSCLE GROUPS**

This is an important exercise for lower back problems and core stabilization. It is a very effective abdominal strengthening exercise.

**BEGINNING PHASE** ▶

1

With the back and sacrum flat on the floor and hands interlocked supporting the head and neck, begin with the legs together and slightly bent at the 10 o'clock position. If the 10 o'clock position puts too much stress on your lower abs, or if you have lower back problems, you might want to start with the knees bent at 90 degrees.

things to avoid

AVOID GOING TOO FAST, SWINGING THE LEGS, AND USING THAT MOMENTUM TO ACCOMPLISH THE MOVEMENT. ALSO, AVOID AN EXCESSIVE RANGE OF MOVEMENT WITH THE LEGS. DON'T EXTEND THE LEGS DOWN TOO FAR AS THIS PUTS A STRAIN ON THE LOWER BACK, AND DON'T CURL THE LEGS UP TOO FAR AS THIS DECREASES THE ISOLATION IN THE ABS AND SHIFTS THE EFFORT TO THE HIP FLEXORS, GREATLY REDUCING THE EFFECTIVENESS OF THE EXERCISE. ALSO AVOID LIFTING UP THE HEAD AND NECK.

**END PHASE**

2

Initiate the move by curling up the hips and then the lower back, lifting the lower back off of the floor. In the end phase the legs should be straight up and you should visualize your feet being pushed straight up toward the ceiling.

3

The return motion should be slow and controlled, visualizing the lower back rolling down one vertebra at a time until the sacrum is again flat on the floor and the legs are back at the 10 o'clock position.

**key points**

FOCUS ON CURLING UP THE HIPS AND LOWER BACK BY USING THE LOWER ABS. DO NOT USE THE MOMENTUM OF THE LEGS TO ACCOMPLISH THIS EXERCISE.

# upper ab roll ups on the
# abdominal bench

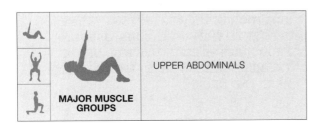

| | |
|---|---|
| MAJOR MUSCLE GROUPS | UPPER ABDOMINALS |

When done properly, this is an effective exercise for lower back stabilization. It is also beneficial for learning to work the deeper layers of the abdominal cavity, thus reducing the waistline and developing the core muscle structures.

**BEGINNING PHASE** ▶

## 1

Adjust the bench to the horizontal position (for a more advanced exercise, you can decline the angle of the bench). Position legs in the leg pads such that the knees are at a right angle.

## 2

Begin with the arms straight out from the chest. Initiate the movement by forcing air out while hollowing out the abdomen (making the belly concave). This is not a straightforward abdominal crunch. By performing it this way, you isolate the transverse abdominals and obliques rather than just using the rectus abdominus muscle to accomplish the movement. This results in using the core muscles and trimming your waistline more effectively.

Continue upward movement, reaching with your fingers straight up to the ceiling. Do not let the fingers (and hands) go forward toward the knees.

**FOCUS ON CURLING UP THE UPPER BODY USING THE UPPER ABS, REMEMBERING TO FORCE AIR OUT AND TO HOLLOW OUT THE STOMACH REGION. DO NOT USE THE MOMENTUM OF THE ARMS AND UPPER BODY TO ACCOMPLISH THIS EXERCISE.**

**AVOID GOING TOO FAST, SWINGING, AND USING THE MOMENTUM OF THE UPPER BODY TO ACCOMPLISH THE MOVEMENT.**

▶ **END PHASE**

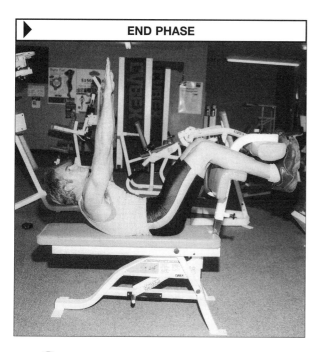

3

The upper body and head should curl up, vertebra by vertebra. Make sure that the chin and head do not lead the movement. Accomplish the movement with the abdominals; do not use the momentum of the upper body and arms.

4

The return motion should be slow and controlled, visualizing the upper back rolling down one vertebra at a time.

# upper ab roll ups off the floor

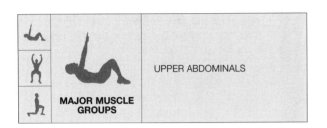

| | UPPER ABDOMINALS |
| MAJOR MUSCLE GROUPS | |

**When done properly, this is an effective exercise for lower back stabilization and learning to work the deeper layers of the abdominal cavity, thus reducing the waistline and developing the core muscle structures.**

**BEGINNING PHASE** ▶

## 1

Position the legs with knees bent and together and feet on the floor. Begin with the arms straight out from the chest.

## 2

Initiate the movement by forcing air out while hollowing out the abdomen (making the belly concave). This is not a straightforward abdominal crunch. By performing it this way, you isolate the transverse abdominals and obliques rather than just using the rectus abdominus muscle to accomplish the movement. This results in using the core muscles and trimming your waistline more effectively.

**FOCUS ON CURLING UP THE UPPER BODY USING THE UPPER ABS, REMEMBERING TO FORCE AIR OUT AND TO HOLLOW OUT THE STOMACH REGION. DO NOT USE THE MOMENTUM OF THE HEAD AND UPPER BODY TO ACCOMPLISH THIS EXERCISE.**

things to avoid

**AVOID GOING TOO FAST, SWINGING, AND USING THE MOMENTUM OF THE HEAD AND UPPER BODY TO ACCOMPLISH THE MOVEMENT.**

▶ **END PHASE**

3

Continue upward movement, reaching with your fingers straight up to the ceiling. Do not let the fingers (and hands) go forward toward the knees.

The upper body and head should curl up, vertebra by vertebra. Make sure that the chin and head do not lead the movement. Accomplish the movement with the abdominals; do not use the momentum of the upper body and arms.

4

The return motion should be slow and controlled, visualizing the upper back rolling down one vertebra at a time.

# cybex® rotary torso

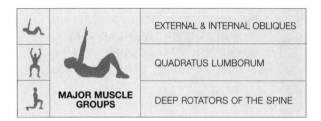

| | | |
|---|---|---|
| | | EXTERNAL & INTERNAL OBLIQUES |
| | | QUADRATUS LUMBORUM |
| | **MAJOR MUSCLE GROUPS** | DEEP ROTATORS OF THE SPINE |

**This is a great exercise for isolating the obliques and rotators of the spine, as well as for increasing the range of motion in the upper torso and lower back region.**

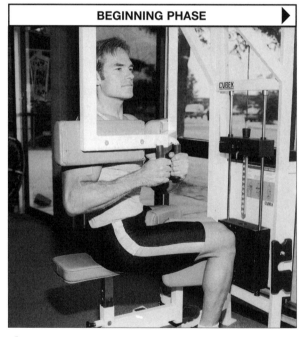

### BEGINNING PHASE ▶

1

Adjust the seat height so that the shoulders are slightly above the chest pads when the upper body is in a full upright posture. The legs should be bent at right angles and should be squeezing the leg pads, engaging the adductors at all times. The head and the sternum should be positioned in the middle of the chest pads throughout the entire range of the movement.

**MAINTAIN UPRIGHT POSTURE AT ALL TIMES. AVOID OVERROTATION OF THE SHOULDERS AND HEAD AND BE SURE TO ISOLATE THE ROTATION FROM THE TORSO.**

things to avoid

**AVOID OVERROTATION OF THE SHOULDERS AND HEAD.**

▶ **END PHASE**

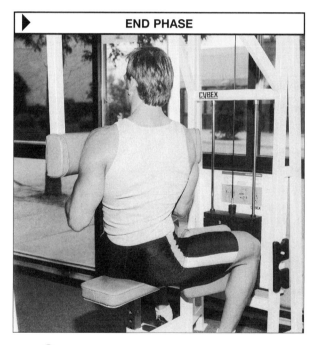

2

Initiate the movement by pushing with the outer hand, not pulling with the inner hand, while focusing on continuing the rotation from the torso and not the shoulders or upper body. It is important to remember to keep the upper body upright during the entire movement. Avoid rotation of the shoulders and head beyond the rotation of the torso.

3

Set the range limiter to a manageable rotation setting for both directions. Remember to keep repetitions equal on both sides, even if one side is stronger than the other.

# cybex® 45-degree angle
## hyperextensions

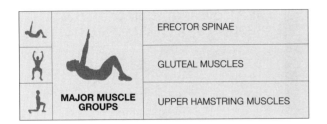

| | | |
|---|---|---|
| | | ERECTOR SPINAE |
| | **MAJOR MUSCLE GROUPS** | GLUTEAL MUSCLES |
| | | UPPER HAMSTRING MUSCLES |

**This is a good lower back, glute, and upper hamstring exercise. However, caution should be exercised if you have lower back problems.**

**BEGINNING PHASE/SIDE VIEW** ▶

1

Adjust the hip support so that it lines up with the pelvis. Position the feet slightly turned out with arms folded across the chest.

**key points**

KEEP THE FEET TURNED OUT,
SQUEEZING THE GLUTES
DURING THE EXTENSION PHASE.

**things to avoid**

AVOID EXCESSIVE RANGE OF
MOTION AND PERFORMING THE
REPETITIONS TOO FAST.

▶ END PHASE/SIDE VIEW   ▶ END PHASE/BACK VIEW

## 2

Begin the movement bent at the waist so that the shoulders are level with the hand grips. Extend the back from the waist using the belt line as the fulcrum point. Continue extension until you achieve 10 to 20 degrees hyperextension. It is important to perform this movement with the back extensors, the gluteal muscles, and the upper hamstrings. Turning your feet out will enable you to squeeze the glutes during the extension phase.

# chapter eleven
# designing your own workout

THINGS YOU WILL LEARN IN THIS CHAPTER:

**PUTTING IT ALL TOGETHER**

**FREQUENCY**

**DURATION**

**WHEN TO INCREASE RESISTANCE—
THE "8-TO-15" RULE**

**VARYING SETS AND REPETITIONS**

**SELECTING BAM SUPERSET™ COMBINATIONS**

**TAILORING YOUR WORKOUT FOR SPECIFIC NEEDS**

**WEEKLY WORKOUT SAMPLES:**
      **THE BEGINNER PROGRAM**
      **THE ADVANCED WEIGHT-LOSS AND TONE PROGRAMS**
      **THE ADVANCED POWER AND STRENGTH PROGRAMS**

# designing your own workout

## PUTTING IT ALL TOGETHER

Now that you've learned the correct technique for all of the exercises in this book, this chapter will teach you how to use them to design your own personal workout.

### FREQUENCY

Depending on your time schedule and workout goals, the frequency of your workouts will vary. In the weekly workout samples contained in this chapter, we present options for resistive weight training at frequencies of two times a week, three times a week, and four times a week. Cardio work should be done daily, with varying intensity and duration.

### DURATION

Weight training sessions should last no longer than 60 minutes. If you are performing intense cardio on a given day, no weight training should be attempted. The reason for the 60-minute limit is that the body only has so much physiological capability (energy reserve) in a 24-hour time period. If you go beyond this limit, you likely will be overtraining, hindering your body's ability to recover.

### WHEN TO INCREASE RESISTANCE—THE "8-TO-15" RULE

Simply put, the "8-to-15" rule is as follows. If you can perform 15 repetitions at a given weight using proper technique and feel that you can easily do more repetitions, then it is time to move to the next weighted increment. In contrast, if you cannot perform 8 repetitions at a given weight with proper technique, you should lower your resistance level.

In addition, a variance in resistance levels should be used. Lighter weights should be used in the warm-up phase, while heavier resistances should be used to obtain the maximum results from each set. For example, when performing a dumbbell curl, 10 pounds might be used as a warm-up in the first set, followed by a set using 15 pounds. If that set was easy, you might follow that with another set using 20-pound dumbbells.

It is extremely important not to sacrifice technique in an attempt to lift too much weight. When increasing the resistance levels, a common mistake is to compensate with other (nontargeted) muscle groups, utilize momentum or speed, and sacrifice correct postural alignment. Any of these compensations can result in reduced isolation of the targeted muscle and can increase the potential for injury. In contrast, too light a weight does not challenge the muscles enough to stimulate growth.

### VARYING SETS AND REPETITIONS

There are two different styles of workouts—power and strength workouts and weight-loss and tone workouts. In the power and strength workout, generally three to five sets of a given exercise are performed, with each set consisting of 6 to 10 repetitions. In the weight-loss and tone workout, usually two or three sets of a given exercise are typically performed, with each set consisting of 12 to 15 repetitions. In either case, the weight used should be determined by one's ability to perform the repetitions with the proper technique.

## SELECTING BAM SUPERSET™ COMBINATIONS

We believe that the most effective way to workout is by using balanced antagonistic muscle group, or BAM, Supersets™. Generally, these consist of alternating exercises that target opposing muscle groups. However, occasionally the BAM Supersets™ will target muscle groups that work synergistically together rather than those that are directly opposing. Combinations of three or more different exercises can be utilized in a BAM Superset™ circuit. Some examples of each of these combinations are listed below and on page 172.

### Opposing Muscle Groups

1. **FRONT PULLDOWN (UPPER BACK) AND DUMBBELL INCLINE PRESS (CHEST).**

2. **CYBEX® VR-2 CHEST PRESS (CHEST) AND CYBEX® ROW (UPPER BACK).**

3. **TRICEP ROPE PULLDOWN (TRICEPS) AND BICEP CURL (BICEPS).**

4. **LEG EXTENSION (QUADRICEPS) AND LEG CURL (HAMSTRINGS).**

5. **HIP ABDUCTION (EXTERNAL HIP ROTATORS) AND HIP ADDUCTION (ADDUCTOR MUSCLES).**

### Synergistic Muscle Groups

1. **ARNOLDS (SHOULDERS) AND SEATED DUMBBELL CURLS (BICEPS).**

2. **CYBEX® OVERHEAD PRESS (SHOULDERS) AND REVERSE FLY (POSTERIOR DELTOID).**

3. **LUNGES (LEGS AND CORE) AND LEG PRESSES (QUADRICEPS AND GLUTES).**

4. **ROTATORS (ROTATOR CUFF MUSCLES) AND DUMBBELL LATERAL RAISES (MEDIAL DELTOID).**

# more bam superset™
## combinations

1. ARNOLDS (SHOULDERS), TRICEP ROPE PULLDOWNS (TRICEPS), AND BICEP CURLS (BICEPS).

2. CYBEX® ROW (UPPER BACK), CYBEX® REVERSE FLY (POSTERIOR DELTOID), AND CYBEX® VR-2 CHEST PRESS (CHEST).

3. CORE CIRCUIT SPECIAL: LUNGES (LEGS AND CORE), SWISS BALL SQUATS (QUADRICEPS AND GLUTES), LOWER/UPPER ABDOMINAL ROLL UPS (ABDOMINALS), HIP ABDUCTION (EXTERNAL HIP ROTATORS), AND HIP ADDUCTION (ADDUCTOR MUSCLES).

4. CORE TORSO SPECIAL: LOWER/UPPER ABDOMINAL ROLL UPS (ABDOMINALS), LOWER BACK HYPEREXTENSIONS (LOWER BACK AND GLUTES), AND ROTARY TORSO (OBLIQUES AND QUADRATUS LUMBORUM).

5. LUNGES (LEGS AND CORE), BUTT BLASTER® (GLUTES AND UPPER HAMSTRINGS), LEG PRESS (QUADRICEPS AND GLUTES), AND SEATED LEG CURLS (HAMSTRINGS).

6. FLAT BENCH PRESS (CHEST), STANDARD LAT FRONT PULLDOWNS (LATISSIMUS DORSI), AND DUMBBELL CURLS (BICEPS).

# TAILORING YOUR WORKOUT FOR SPECIFIC NEEDS

The workout samples that we provide in this chapter address the three general workout programs that most individuals might utilize. However, we know from experience that many situations will require some modification to the workouts. Below are common questions we have encountered over the years and our general guidance in response.

**Q: I have neck and shoulder pain; will working out help or should I avoid working out?**

A: Of course with any injury, you should consult your doctor or health care professional before beginning any exercise program. Provided you do not have a tear in a muscle or tendon or a disk or neurological problem, an appropriate lifting and exercise program can be beneficial for both neck and shoulder injuries.

For both neck and shoulder problems, you must first develop a functional and stable sternal–scapular relationship. This can be accomplished by training the mid- and lower scapular muscle groups in combination with lengthening and mobilization of the chest muscles.

In most situations where there are injuries in the shoulders and neck, the body tends to immobilize these regions and compensate by using the upper traps to protect and guard the injury sites. The result is a limited range of motion with the sternum collapsed and the shoulders hunched and rolled forward. To correct this musculoskeletal imbalance, mobility to the scapular and sternal regions must be restored.

A combination of row and pulldown movements supersetted with light chest exercises will work best to generate mobility and stability in the sternal and scapular regions. Examples of these BAM Supersets are: Cybex row and Cybex chest press, and front pulldowns and dumbbell incline press. The keys to correctly performing these exercises include developing the ability to open and uplift the chest while at the same time "anchoring" your shoulder blades.

"Anchoring" the shoulder blades (scapulae) involves retraction and downward rotation using the rhomboids, middle traps, and lower traps. These muscles are trained with the rowing and pulldown exercises. It is also important to anchor the shoulder blades when doing any upper body exercise, particularly overhead and pushing movements.

Once you have mastered the ability to anchor the shoulder blades both as a prime mover (rows and pulldowns) and as a stabilizer (presses and pushes) and are no longer experiencing pain in the shoulders and neck, the next step is to advance to overhead and heavier push movements.

**Q: I have lower back pain; will working out help or should I avoid working out?**

A: Always consult your doctor or health care professional before beginning any exercise program if you have any injury. Provided you do not have a severe disk or neurological problem, weight lifting and exercise can be very beneficial, helping to alleviate lower back pain.

When beginning an exercise program, the first step should be developing a core awareness by training the abdominal muscles along with working the hip abductors and adductors. Hamstring strength and flexibility are also important in lower back stabilization. For this, we recommend the seated leg curl machine, as it produces less stress on the lower back than the prone leg curl machine. You should also do the one-legged hamstring stretch throughout the workout as well as throughout the day. Tight piriformis and gluteal muscles can also contribute to lower back pain. Thus, the glute and piriformis stretch is effective as well.

After several weeks of developing your core awareness and achieving greater flexibility in the hamstrings and glutes, progress to more functionally integrated moves. We do not recommend any compressive lifts such as heavy plate-loaded leg presses or bar squats that compress the spine. However, we strongly recommend lunges and Swiss Ball squats. It should be noted that you may want to avoid the lower back hyperextension exercise, as this can produce too much pressure (compression) on the lumbar spine.

**Q: If I do enough outdoors for my lower body—running, hiking, skiing—can I just train my upper body?**

A: Since most outdoor and cardio activities are by nature endurance and aerobic activities, specific lower body muscle groups often become imbalanced or are undertrained. For example, in running and biking, the quadriceps and hip flexors are often overdeveloped relative to the hamstrings, abductors, and adductors. In addition, strength and power do not get developed to their full

potential. By training the lower body with weights, it is possible to improve outdoor activities and sports performance. Therefore, we recommend lower body weight training at least once per week.

**Q: I have knee problems; will working out help or should I avoid training my lower body?**

A: With any injury, consult your doctor or health care professional before beginning any exercise program. If you do not have a severe problem, such as a torn ligament or excessive damage to the cartilage, specific weight training exercises can help stabilize your knee.

Initially, develop stability and strength around the knee joint by training the hamstrings, hip abductors, hip adductors, and calf muscles. Cardiovascular endurance is also key, but the choice of a proper cardio exercise depends on how the knee responds.

Flexibility in the hamstrings, tensor fascia latae (TFL), iliotibial (IT) band, and, sometimes, the quadricep muscles can also help in knee stabilization and pain reduction. For this, the one-legged hamstring stretch, the psoas stretch, and the glute and piriformis stretch are recommended. These stretches can be done throughout a workout as well as throughout the day.

Development of quadricep muscle group strength, in particular the vastus medialis and vastus lateralis lower insertions, will help in overall knee stabilization. The best way to achieve this is with quadricep exercises that do not irritate or overly stress the knee joint. In general, avoid full range and heavy leg extensions. The leg extension exercise can be effective in isolating the vastus medialis and vastus lateralis muscles when limiting the range of motion to the final 30 degrees of extension and keeping the weight relatively light.

Effective lower body strength exercises that can be done with knee problems are: the Cybex leg press; the Swiss Ball squat; and, after sufficiently stabilizing the knee joint, the dumbbell lunge. However, if the knee becomes irritated, these exercises should be discontinued.

# the beginner
## program

## THE BEGINNER PROGRAM

This is a program designed for those who have never been involved in a strength training program or who have never done one consistently. The program is designed to build a solid strength base, allowing you to gain confidence and to attain the proper lifting technique. Consistency and the ability to focus on the correct muscles being trained are an integral part of this beginning phase. We recommend staying with this beginning program consistently for the first 6 to 12 weeks.

In the first couple of weeks, the most important issue is not the amount of weight or resistance, but rather that correct technique is used in each exercise. Once the correct technique is mastered, use the "8-to-15" rule previously outlined to determine the appropriate amount of weight or resistance. Remember: Never sacrifice technique for more weight.

In the four-week sample schedule provided, we have emphasized an overall, full-body workout divided into two weekly workouts. In addition, it is important to include the recommended cardio exercises and pay attention to nutrition (pre- and postworkout meals).

| key points | CONSISTENCY, CORRECT TECHNIQUE, AND BUILDING A SOLID STRENGTH BASE. |
|---|---|

**BEGINNER PROGRAM SAMPLE MONDAY THROUGH SATURDAY**
WEEK ONE

| MONDAY | TUESDAY | WEDNESDAY | THURSDAY | FRIDAY | SATURDAY | SUNDAY |
|---|---|---|---|---|---|---|
| 11:00 am<br>PREWORKOUT MEAL<br>Eat light, healthy carbs and proteins.<br><br>12:00 pm<br>WEIGHT TRAINING<br>Warm-up<br>5 minutes<br>on the bike.<br><br>**SUPERSET**<br>**2 sets x 15 reps each**<br>• Cybex® Chest<br>• Cybex® Row<br><br>**SUPERSET**<br>**2 sets x 15 reps each**<br>• Front Pulldowns<br>• Arnolds<br><br>**SUPERSET**<br>**2 sets x 15 reps each**<br>• Hip Abduction<br>• Hip Adduction<br><br>**SOLO EXERCISE**<br>**2 sets x 10 reps**<br>• Lower Ab Roll Ups<br><br>5 minutes elliptical machine<br>15 minutes treadmill<br><br>2:00 pm<br>POSTWORKOUT MEAL<br>Eat healthy, high protein with carbs. | Walk 30 minutes<br>LOW INTENSITY | Walk 30 minutes<br>LOW INTENSITY | 11:00 am<br>PREWORKOUT MEAL<br>Eat light, healthy carbs and proteins.<br><br>12:00 pm<br>WEIGHT TRAINING<br>Warm-up<br>5 minutes<br>on the bike.<br><br>**SUPERSET**<br>**2 sets x 15 reps each**<br>• Cybex® Chest<br>• Cybex® Row<br><br>**SUPERSET**<br>**2 sets x 15 reps each**<br>• Front Pulldowns<br>• Arnolds<br><br>**SUPERSET**<br>**2 sets x 15 reps each**<br>• Hip Abduction<br>• Hip Adduction<br><br>**SOLO EXERCISE**<br>**2 sets x 10 reps**<br>• Lower Ab Roll Ups<br><br>5 minutes elliptical machine<br>15 minutes treadmill<br><br>2:00 pm<br>POSTWORKOUT MEAL<br>Eat healthy, high protein with carbs. | Walk 30 minutes<br>LOW INTENSITY | Walk 30 minutes<br>LOW INTENSITY | REST |

## BEGINNER PROGRAM SAMPLE MONDAY THROUGH SATURDAY
WEEK TWO

| MONDAY | TUESDAY | WEDNESDAY | THURSDAY | FRIDAY | SATURDAY | SUNDAY |
|---|---|---|---|---|---|---|
| 11:00 am<br>PREWORKOUT MEAL<br>Eat light, healthy carbs and proteins.<br><br>12:00 pm<br>WEIGHT TRAINING<br>Warm-up<br>5 minutes on the bike.<br><br>**SUPERSET**<br>**2 sets x 15 reps each**<br>• Cybex® Chest<br>• Cybex® Row<br><br>**SUPERSET**<br>**2 sets x 15 reps each**<br>• Front Pulldowns<br>• Dumbbell Incline Press<br><br>**SUPERSET**<br>**2 sets x 15 reps each**<br>• Arnolds<br>• Seated Dumbbell Curls<br><br>**SUPERSET CIRCUIT**<br>**2 sets x 15 reps each**<br>• Hip Abduction<br>• Hip Adduction<br>• Seated Leg Curls<br><br>**SOLO EXERCISE**<br>**2 sets x 12 reps**<br>• Lower Ab Roll Ups<br><br>8 minutes elliptical machine<br>10 minutes treadmill<br><br>2:00 pm<br>POSTWORKOUT MEAL<br>Eat healthy, high protein with carbs. | 10 minutes elliptical machine<br>20 minutes treadmill<br>LOW INTENSITY | Walk or bike<br>30 minutes<br>LOW INTENSITY | 11:00 am<br>PREWORKOUT MEAL<br>Eat light, healthy carbs and proteins.<br><br>12:00 pm<br>WEIGHT TRAINING<br>Warm-up<br>5 minutes on the bike.<br><br>**SUPERSET**<br>**2 sets x 15 reps each**<br>• Cybex® Chest<br>• Cybex® Row<br><br>**SUPERSET**<br>**2 sets x 15 reps each**<br>• Front Pulldowns<br>• Dumbbell Incline Press<br><br>**SUPERSET**<br>**2 sets x 15 reps each**<br>• Arnolds<br>• Seated Dumbbell Curls<br><br>**SUPERSET CIRCUIT**<br>**2 sets x 15 reps each**<br>• Hip Abduction<br>• Hip Adduction<br>• Seated Leg Curls<br><br>**SOLO EXERCISE**<br>**2 sets x 12 reps**<br>• Lower Ab Roll Ups<br><br>8 minutes elliptical machine<br>10 minutes treadmill<br><br>2:00 pm<br>POSTWORKOUT MEAL<br>Eat healthy, high protein with carbs. | 10 minutes elliptical machine<br>20 minutes treadmill<br>LOW INTENSITY | Walk 30 minutes<br>LOW INTENSITY | REST |

## BEGINNER PROGRAM SAMPLE MONDAY THROUGH SATURDAY
### WEEK THREE

| MONDAY | TUESDAY | WEDNESDAY | THURSDAY | FRIDAY | SATURDAY | SUNDAY |
|---|---|---|---|---|---|---|
| 11:00 am<br>PREWORKOUT MEAL<br>Eat light, healthy carbs and proteins.<br><br>12:00 pm<br>WEIGHT TRAINING<br>Warm-up<br>5 minutes<br>on the bike.<br><br>**SUPERSET**<br>**2 sets x 15 reps each**<br>• Cybex® Chest<br>• Cybex® Row<br><br>**SUPERSET**<br>**2 sets x 15 reps each**<br>• Front Pulldowns<br>• Dumbbell Incline Press<br><br>**SUPERSET**<br>**2 sets x 15 reps each**<br>• Rotators<br>• Dumbbell Lateral Raises<br><br>**SUPERSET CIRCUIT**<br>**2 sets x 15 reps each**<br>• Cybex® Leg Press<br>• Seated Leg Curls<br>• Lower Ab Roll Ups<br><br>**SOLO EXERCISE**<br>**2 sets x 15 reps**<br>• Lower Ab Roll Ups<br><br>8 minutes elliptical machine<br>12 minutes treadmill<br><br>2:00 pm<br>POSTWORKOUT MEAL<br>Eat healthy, high protein with carbs. | 10 minutes elliptical machine<br>20 minutes treadmill<br>LOW INTENSITY | Walk or bike 30 minutes<br>LOW INTENSITY | 11:00 am<br>PREWORKOUT MEAL<br>Eat light, healthy carbs and proteins.<br><br>12:00 pm<br>WEIGHT TRAINING<br>Warm-up<br>5 minutes<br>on the bike.<br><br>**SUPERSET**<br>**2 sets x 15 reps each**<br>• Cybex® Chest<br>• Cybex® Row<br><br>**SUPERSET**<br>**2 sets x 15 reps each**<br>• Front Pulldowns<br>• Dumbbell Incline Press<br><br>**SUPERSET**<br>**2 sets x 15 reps each**<br>• Rotators<br>• Dumbbell Lateral Raises<br><br>**SUPERSET CIRCUIT**<br>**2 sets x 15 reps each**<br>• Cybex® Leg Press<br>• Seated Leg Curls<br>• Lower Ab Roll Ups<br><br>**SOLO EXERCISE**<br>**2 sets x 15 reps**<br>• Lower Ab Roll Ups<br><br>8 minutes elliptical machine<br>12 minutes treadmill<br><br>2:00 pm<br>POSTWORKOUT MEAL<br>Eat healthy, high protein with carbs. | 10 minutes elliptical machine<br>20 minutes treadmill<br>LOW INTENSITY | Walk 30 minutes<br>LOW INTENSITY | REST |

**BEGINNER PROGRAM SAMPLE MONDAY THROUGH SATURDAY**
WEEK FOUR

| MONDAY | TUESDAY | WEDNESDAY | THURSDAY | FRIDAY | SATURDAY | SUNDAY |
|---|---|---|---|---|---|---|
| 11:00 am<br>PREWORKOUT MEAL<br>Eat light, healthy carbs and proteins.<br><br>12:00 pm<br>WEIGHT TRAINING<br>Warm-up<br>5 minutes<br>on the bike.<br><br>**SUPERSET**<br>**2 sets x 15 reps each**<br>• Cybex® Chest Advanced Move<br>• Cybex® Row<br><br>**SUPERSET**<br>**2 sets x 15 reps each**<br>• Front Pulldowns<br>• Dumbbell Incline Press<br><br>**SUPERSET**<br>**2 sets x 15 reps each**<br>• Cybex® Overhead Press<br>• Cybex® Reverse Fly<br><br>**SUPERSET CIRCUIT**<br>**3 sets x 15 reps each**<br>• Cybex® Leg Press<br>• Seated Leg Curls<br>• Lower Ab Roll Ups<br><br>10 minutes elliptical machine<br>15 minutes treadmill<br><br>2:00 pm<br>POSTWORKOUT MEAL<br>Eat healthy, high protein with carbs. | 12 minutes elliptical machine<br>20 minutes treadmill<br>LOW INTENSITY | Walk or bike<br>30 minutes<br>LOW INTENSITY | 11:00 am<br>PREWORKOUT MEAL<br>Eat light, healthy carbs and proteins.<br><br>12:00 pm<br>WEIGHT TRAINING<br>Warm-up<br>5 minutes<br>on the bike.<br><br>**SUPERSET**<br>**2 sets x 15 reps each**<br>• Cybex® Chest Advanced Move<br>• Cybex® Row<br><br>**SUPERSET**<br>**2 sets x 15 reps each**<br>• Front Pulldowns<br>• Dumbbell Incline Press<br><br>**SUPERSET**<br>**2 sets x 15 reps each**<br>• Cybex® Overhead Press<br>• Cybex® Reverse Fly<br><br>**SUPERSET CIRCUIT**<br>**3 sets x 15 reps each**<br>• Cybex® Leg Press<br>• Seated Leg Curls<br>• Lower Ab Roll Ups<br><br>10 minutes elliptical machine<br>15 minutes treadmill<br><br>2:00 pm<br>POSTWORKOUT MEAL<br>Eat healthy, high protein with carbs. | 12 minutes elliptical machine<br>20 minutes treadmill<br>LOW INTENSITY | Walk 30 minutes<br>LOW INTENSITY | REST |

# weight-loss and the advanced tone programs

This program is designed for anyone who wants strength without bulk. In addition to building strength, this program targets areas to be toned and firmed that are typically loose and flabby. While it is not possible to target fat loss at specific sites, it is possible to target muscles or muscle groups to firm specific sites. This approach typically utilizes a high number of repetitions (12 to 15) and two or three BAM Supersets targeting a specific area.

Cardio exercise is emphasized in this program. Please note that this does not mean to overtrain when doing cardio. It is important to limit your intense cardio to twice a week. It is also important to be consistent with performing cardio exercises daily as outlined.

A healthy and balanced diet is instrumental to weight-loss and tone programs. Individuals sometimes have a tendency to undereat, thus sending their body into "survival mode," resulting in increased fat storage and destruction of muscle tissue. Remember to provide your body with proper nutrients, including adequate protein and good carbs. The pre- and postworkout meals are extremely important.

In the four-week workout layouts outlined below, we have included samples for strength training at a frequency of two, three, and four times a week. The two times a week schedule will typically allow you to maintain current levels of strength and muscle tone. The three times a week schedule will allow you to improve current levels and achieve your goals more readily. The four times a week schedule is for when you are seeking more strength and overall muscle tone and definition.

| key points | CONSISTENCY, CORRECT TECHNIQUE, HIGHER REPETITIONS, INCREASED CARDIO, AND QUALITY NUTRITION. |
|---|---|

## ADVANCED WEIGHT-LOSS AND TONE PROGRAM SAMPLE 2x a week
WEEK ONE

| MONDAY | TUESDAY | WEDNESDAY | THURSDAY | FRIDAY | SATURDAY | SUNDAY |
|---|---|---|---|---|---|---|
| 11:00 am<br>PREWORKOUT MEAL<br>Eat light, healthy carbs and proteins.<br><br>12:00 pm<br>WEIGHT TRAINING<br>Warm-up<br>5 minutes<br>on the bike.<br><br>**SUPERSET CIRCUIT**<br>**2 sets x 15 reps each**<br>• Cybex® Chest Advanced Move<br>• Cybex® Row<br>• Cybex® Reverse Fly<br><br>**SUPERSET**<br>**2 sets x 15 reps each**<br>• Hammer Front Pulldowns<br>• Dumbbell Incline Press<br><br>**SUPERSET**<br>**2 sets x 15 reps each**<br>• Hip Abduction<br>• Hip Adduction<br><br>**SUPERSET CIRCUIT**<br>**2 sets x 15 reps each**<br>• Lunges<br>• Butt Blaster®<br>• Leg Press<br>• Seated Leg Curls<br><br>**SUPERSET CIRCUIT**<br>**2 sets x 20 reps each**<br>• Lower Ab Roll Ups<br>• Upper Ab Roll Ups<br>• Rotary Torso<br><br>10 minutes elliptical machine 20 minutes treadmill<br><br>2:00 pm<br>POSTWORKOUT MEAL<br>Eat healthy, high protein with carbs. | Spinning, aerobics, or elliptical machine (no longer than 45 minutes)<br>HIGH INTENSITY | Walk or bike 45 minutes<br>LOW INTENSITY | 11:00 am<br>PREWORKOUT MEAL<br>Eat light, healthy carbs and proteins.<br><br>12:00 pm<br>WEIGHT TRAINING<br>Warm-up<br>5 minutes<br>on the bike.<br><br>**SUPERSET CIRCUIT**<br>**2 sets x 15 reps each**<br>• Cybex® Chest Advanced Move<br>• Cybex® Row<br>• Cybex® Reverse Fly<br><br>**SUPERSET CIRCUIT**<br>**2 sets x 15 reps each**<br>• Arnolds<br>• Seated Dumbbell Curls<br>• Tricep Rope Pulldowns<br><br>**SUPERSET CIRCUIT**<br>**2 sets x 15 reps each**<br>• Hip Abduction<br>• Hip Adduction<br>• Seated Leg Curls<br><br>**SUPERSET CIRCUIT**<br>**2 sets x 20 reps each**<br>• Lower Ab Roll Ups<br>• Upper Ab Roll Ups<br>• Rotary Torso<br><br>10 minutes elliptical machine 20 minutes treadmill<br><br>2:00 pm<br>POSTWORKOUT MEAL<br>Eat healthy, high protein with carbs. | Spinning, aerobics, or elliptical machine (no longer than 45 minutes)<br>HIGH INTENSITY | Walk or bike 45 minutes<br>LOW INTENSITY | Walk 30 minutes<br>LOW INTENSITY |

## ADVANCED WEIGHT-LOSS AND TONE PROGRAM SAMPLE 2x a week
### WEEK TWO

| MONDAY | TUESDAY | WEDNESDAY | THURSDAY | FRIDAY | SATURDAY | SUNDAY |
|---|---|---|---|---|---|---|
| 11:00 am<br>PREWORKOUT MEAL<br>Eat light, healthy carbs and proteins.<br><br>12:00 pm<br>WEIGHT TRAINING<br>Warm-up<br>5 minutes<br>on the bike.<br><br>**SUPERSET**<br>**2 sets x 15 reps each**<br>• "Pec-Dec" Chest Fly<br>• "Pec-Dec" Reverse Fly<br><br>**SUPERSET**<br>**2 sets x 15 reps each**<br>• Hammer Front Pulldowns<br>• Dumbbell Incline Press<br><br>**SUPERSET CIRCUIT**<br>**2 sets x 15 reps each**<br>• Leg Extensions<br>• Prone Leg Curls<br>• Rotary Calf Machine<br><br>**SUPERSET CIRCUIT**<br>**2 sets x 15 reps each**<br>• Hip Abduction<br>• Hip Adduction<br>• Butt Blaster®<br><br>**SUPERSET CIRCUIT**<br>**2 sets x 20 reps each**<br>• Lower Ab Roll Ups<br>• Upper Ab Roll Ups<br>• Rotary Torso<br><br>10 minutes elliptical machine 20 minutes treadmill<br><br>2:00 pm<br>POSTWORKOUT MEAL<br>Eat healthy, high protein with carbs. | Spinning, aerobics, or elliptical machine (no longer than 45 minutes)<br>HIGH INTENSITY | Walk or bike 45 minutes<br>LOW INTENSITY | 11:00 am<br>PREWORKOUT MEAL<br>Eat light, healthy carbs and proteins.<br><br>12:00 pm<br>WEIGHT TRAINING<br>Warm-up<br>5 minutes<br>on the bike.<br><br>**SUPERSET CIRCUIT**<br>**2 sets x 15 reps each**<br>• Cybex® Chest Advanced Move<br>• Cybex® Row<br>• Cybex® Reverse Fly<br><br>**SUPERSET CIRCUIT**<br>**2 sets x 15 reps each**<br>• Arnolds<br>• Seated Dumbbell Curls<br>• Tricep Rope Pulldowns<br><br>**SUPERSET**<br>**2 sets x 15 reps each**<br>• Rotators<br>• Dumbbell Lateral Raises<br><br>**SUPERSET CIRCUIT**<br>**2 sets x 15 reps each**<br>• Hip Abduction<br>• Hip Adduction<br>• Butt Blaster®<br><br>**SUPERSET CIRCUIT**<br>**2 sets x 20 reps each**<br>• Lower Ab Roll Ups<br>• Upper Ab Roll Ups<br>• Rotary Torso<br><br>10 minutes elliptical machine 20 minutes treadmill<br><br>2:00 pm<br>POSTWORKOUT MEAL<br>Eat healthy, high protein with carbs. | Spinning, aerobics, or elliptical machine (no longer than 45 minutes)<br>HIGH INTENSITY | Walk or bike 45 minutes<br>LOW INTENSITY | Walk 30 minutes<br>LOW INTENSITY |

## ADVANCED WEIGHT-LOSS AND TONE PROGRAM SAMPLE 2x a week
WEEK THREE

| MONDAY | TUESDAY | WEDNESDAY | THURSDAY | FRIDAY | SATURDAY | SUNDAY |
|---|---|---|---|---|---|---|
| 11:00 am<br>PREWORKOUT MEAL<br>Eat light, healthy carbs and proteins.<br><br>12:00 pm<br>WEIGHT TRAINING<br>Warm-up<br>5 minutes<br>on the bike.<br><br>**SUPERSET CIRCUIT**<br>**2 sets x 15 reps each**<br>• Cybex® Chest Advanced Move<br>• Cybex® Row<br>• Cybex® Reverse Fly<br><br>**SUPERSET**<br>**2 sets x 15 reps each**<br>• Close Grip Front Pulldowns<br>• "Pec-Dec" Chest Fly<br><br>**SUPERSET**<br>**2 sets x 15 reps each**<br>• Hip Abduction<br>• Hip Adduction<br><br>**SUPERSET CIRCUIT**<br>**2 sets x 15 reps each**<br>• Lunges<br>• Butt Blaster®<br>• Swiss Ball Squats<br>• Seated Leg Curls<br><br>**SUPERSET CIRCUIT**<br>**2 sets x 20 reps each**<br>• Lower Ab Roll Ups<br>• Upper Ab Roll Ups<br>• Rotary Torso<br><br>15 minutes<br>elliptical machine<br>15 minutes treadmill<br><br>2:00 pm<br>POSTWORKOUT MEAL<br>Eat healthy, high protein with carbs. | Spinning, aerobics, or elliptical machine (no longer than 45 minutes)<br>HIGH INTENSITY | Walk or bike<br>45 minutes<br>LOW INTENSITY | 11:00 am<br>PREWORKOUT MEAL<br>Eat light, healthy carbs and proteins.<br><br>12:00 pm<br>WEIGHT TRAINING<br>Warm-up<br>5 minutes<br>on the bike.<br><br>**SUPERSET**<br>**3 sets x 15 reps each**<br>• Incline Dumbbell Press<br>• Hammer Front Pulldowns<br><br>**SUPERSET CIRCUIT**<br>**2 sets x 15 reps each**<br>• Arnolds<br>• Seated Dumbbell Curls<br>• Tricep Rope Pulldowns<br><br>**SUPERSET CIRCUIT**<br>**2 sets x 15 reps each**<br>• Cybex® Overhead Press<br>• Cybex® Arm Curl Machine<br>• Tricep Rope Pulldowns<br><br>**SUPERSET CIRCUIT**<br>**2 sets x 15 reps each**<br>• Hip Abduction<br>• Hip Adduction<br>• Seated Leg Curls<br><br>**SUPERSET CIRCUIT**<br>**2 sets x 20 reps each**<br>• Lower Ab Roll Ups<br>• Upper Ab Roll Ups<br>• Rotary Torso<br><br>15 minutes<br>elliptical machine<br>15 minutes treadmill<br><br>2:00 pm<br>POSTWORKOUT MEAL<br>Eat healthy, high protein with carbs. | Spinning, aerobics, or elliptical machine (no longer than 45 minutes)<br>HIGH INTENSITY | Walk or bike<br>45 minutes<br>LOW INTENSITY | Walk 30 minutes<br>LOW INTENSITY |

**ADVANCED WEIGHT-LOSS AND TONE PROGRAM SAMPLE 2x a week**
WEEK FOUR

| MONDAY | TUESDAY | WEDNESDAY | THURSDAY | FRIDAY | SATURDAY | SUNDAY |
|---|---|---|---|---|---|---|
| 11:00 am<br>PREWORKOUT MEAL<br>Eat light, healthy carbs and proteins. | | | 11:00 am<br>PREWORKOUT MEAL<br>Eat light, healthy carbs and proteins. | | | |
| 12:00 pm<br>WEIGHT TRAINING<br>Warm-up<br>5 minutes<br>on the bike. | | | 12:00 pm<br>WEIGHT TRAINING<br>Warm-up<br>5 minutes<br>on the bike. | | | |
| **SUPERSET**<br>**2 sets x 15 reps each**<br>• "Pec-Dec" Chest Fly<br>• "Pec-Dec" Reverse Fly | | | **SUPERSET**<br>**2 sets x 15 reps each**<br>• Cybex® Chest<br>• Cybex® Row<br>  Advanced Move | | | |
| **SUPERSET**<br>**2 sets x 15 reps each**<br>• Incline Dumbbell Press<br>• Hammer Front Pulldowns | | | **SUPERSET CIRCUIT**<br>**2 sets x 15 reps each**<br>• Cybex® Overhead Press<br>• Cybex® Reverse Fly<br>• Arm Curl Machine | | | |
| **SUPERSET CIRCUIT**<br>**2 sets x 15 reps each**<br>• Leg Extensions<br>• Prone Leg Curls<br>• Rotary Calf Machine | Spinning, aerobics, or elliptical machine (no longer than 45 minutes)<br>HIGH INTENSITY | Walk or bike 45 minutes<br>LOW INTENSITY | **SUPERSET CIRCUIT**<br>**2 sets x 15 reps each**<br>• Arnolds<br>• Seated Dumbbell Curls<br>• Tricep Rope Pulldowns | Spinning, aerobics, or elliptical machine (no longer than 45 minutes)<br>HIGH INTENSITY | Walk or bike 45 minutes<br>LOW INTENSITY | Walk 30 minutes<br>LOW INTENSITY |
| **SUPERSET CIRCUIT**<br>**2 sets x 15 reps each**<br>• Hip Abduction<br>• Hip Adduction<br>• Butt Blaster®<br>• Swiss Ball Squats | | | **SUPERSET**<br>**2 sets x 15 reps each**<br>• Rotators<br>• Dumbbell Lateral Raises | | | |
| **SUPERSET CIRCUIT**<br>**2 sets x 20 reps each**<br>• Lower Ab Roll Ups<br>• Upper Ab Roll Ups<br>• Rotary Torso | | | **SUPERSET CIRCUIT**<br>**2 sets x 15 reps each**<br>• Hip Abduction<br>• Hip Adduction<br>• Seated Leg Curls | | | |
| 15 minutes treadmill | | | **SUPERSET CIRCUIT**<br>**2 sets x 20 reps each**<br>• Lower Ab Roll Ups<br>• Upper Ab Roll Ups<br>• Rotary Torso | | | |
| 2:00 pm<br>POSTWORKOUT MEAL<br>Eat healthy, high protein with carbs. | | | 15 minutes elliptical machine<br>15 minutes treadmill | | | |
| | | | 2:00 pm<br>POSTWORKOUT MEAL<br>Eat healthy, high protein with carbs. | | | |

## ADVANCED WEIGHT-LOSS AND TONE PROGRAM SAMPLE 3x a week
WEEK ONE

| MONDAY | TUESDAY | WEDNESDAY | THURSDAY | FRIDAY | SATURDAY | SUNDAY |
|---|---|---|---|---|---|---|
| 11:00 am<br>PREWORKOUT MEAL<br>Eat light, healthy carbs and proteins. | | 11:00 am<br>PREWORKOUT MEAL<br>Eat light, healthy carbs and proteins. | | 11:00 am<br>PREWORKOUT MEAL<br>Eat light, healthy carbs and proteins. | | |
| 12:00 pm<br>WEIGHT TRAINING<br>Warm-up<br>5 minutes<br>on the bike. | | 12:00 pm<br>WEIGHT TRAINING<br>Warm-up<br>5 minutes<br>on the bike. | | 12:00 pm<br>WEIGHT TRAINING<br>Warm-up<br>5 minutes<br>on the bike. | | |
| **SUPERSET CIRCUIT**<br>**2 sets x 15 reps each**<br>• Cybex® Chest Advanced Move<br>• Cybex® Row<br>• Cybex® Reverse Fly<br><br>**SUPERSET**<br>**2 sets x 15 reps each**<br>• Hammer Front Pulldowns<br>• Dumbbell Incline Press<br><br>**SUPERSET**<br>**2 sets x 15 reps each**<br>• Hip Abduction<br>• Hip Adduction<br><br>**SUPERSET CIRCUIT**<br>**3 sets x 15 reps each**<br>• Lunges<br>• Butt Blaster®<br>• Seated Leg Press<br>• Seated Leg Curls<br><br>**SUPERSET CIRCUIT**<br>**2 sets x 20 reps each**<br>• Lower Ab Roll Ups<br>• Upper Ab Roll Ups<br>• Rotary Torso | Spinning, aerobics, or elliptical machine (no longer than 45 minutes)<br>HIGH INTENSITY | **SUPERSET CIRCUIT**<br>**3 sets x 15 reps each**<br>• Arnolds<br>• Seated Dumbbell Curls<br>• Tricep Rope Pulldowns<br><br>**SUPERSET**<br>**3 sets x 15 reps each**<br>• Rotators<br>• Dumbbell Lateral Raises<br><br>**SUPERSET**<br>**3 sets x 15 reps each**<br>• Cybex® Overhead Press<br>• Cybex® Reverse Fly<br><br>**SUPERSET**<br>**3 sets x 15 reps each**<br>• Cybex® Arm Curl Machine<br>• Tricep Rope Pulldowns<br><br>**SUPERSET CIRCUIT**<br>**2 sets x 20 reps each**<br>• Lower Ab Roll Ups<br>• Upper Ab Roll Ups<br>• Rotary Torso | Run, hike, or bike<br>45 minutes<br>MODERATE INTENSITY | **SUPERSET**<br>**2 sets x 15 reps each**<br>• Cybex® Chest<br>• Cybex® Row Advanced Move<br><br>**SUPERSET**<br>**2 sets x 15 reps each**<br>• "Pec-Dec" Chest Fly<br>• Close Grip Front Pulldowns<br><br>**SUPERSET**<br>**2 sets x 15 reps each**<br>• Dumbbell Incline Press<br>• Wide Grip Front Pulldowns<br><br>**SUPERSET**<br>**2 sets x 15 reps each**<br>• Swiss Ball Squats<br>• Butt Blaster®<br><br>**SUPERSET CIRCUIT**<br>**2 sets x 15 reps each**<br>• Hip Abduction<br>• Hip Adduction<br>• Seated Leg Curls<br><br>**SUPERSET CIRCUIT**<br>**2 sets x 20 reps each**<br>• Lower Ab Roll Ups<br>• Upper Ab Roll Ups<br>• Rotary Torso | Run, hike, or bike<br>45 minutes<br>MODERATE INTENSITY | Walk or bike<br>45 minutes<br>LOW INTENSITY |
| 10 minutes elliptical machine<br>20 minutes treadmill | | 10 minutes elliptical machine<br>20 minutes treadmill | | 10 minutes elliptical machine<br>20 minutes treadmill | | |
| 2:00 pm<br>POSTWORKOUT MEAL<br>Eat healthy, high protein with carbs. | | 2:00 pm<br>POSTWORKOUT MEAL<br>Eat healthy, high protein with carbs. | | 2:00 pm<br>POSTWORKOUT MEAL<br>Eat healthy, high protein with carbs. | | |

## ADVANCED WEIGHT-LOSS AND TONE PROGRAM SAMPLE 3x a week
### WEEK TWO

| MONDAY | TUESDAY | WEDNESDAY | THURSDAY | FRIDAY | SATURDAY | SUNDAY |
|---|---|---|---|---|---|---|
| 11:00 am<br>PREWORKOUT MEAL<br>Eat light, healthy carbs and proteins.<br><br>12:00 pm<br>WEIGHT TRAINING<br>Warm-up<br>5 minutes<br>on the bike.<br><br>**SUPERSET CIRCUIT**<br>**2 sets x 15 reps each**<br>• Cybex® Chest Advanced Move<br>• Cybex® Row<br>• Cybex® Reverse Fly<br><br>**SUPERSET**<br>**2 sets x 15 reps each**<br>• Hammer Front Pulldowns<br>• Dumbbell Incline Press<br><br>**SUPERSET**<br>**2 sets x 15 reps each**<br>• Hip Abduction<br>• Hip Adduction<br><br>**SUPERSET**<br>**2 sets x 15 reps each**<br>• Leg Extensions<br>• Prone Leg Curls<br><br>**SUPERSET CIRCUIT**<br>**3 sets x 15 reps each**<br>• Lunges<br>• Butt Blaster®<br>• Swiss Ball Squats<br>• Seated Leg Curls<br><br>**SUPERSET CIRCUIT**<br>**2 sets x 20 reps each**<br>• Lower Ab Roll Ups<br>• Upper Ab Roll Ups<br>• Rotary Torso<br><br>10 minutes<br>elliptical machine<br>20 minutes treadmill<br><br>2:00 pm<br>POSTWORKOUT MEAL<br>Eat healthy, high protein with carbs. | Spinning, aerobics, or elliptical machine (no longer than 45 minutes)<br>HIGH INTENSITY | 11:00 am<br>PREWORKOUT MEAL<br>Eat light, healthy carbs and proteins.<br><br>12:00 pm<br>WEIGHT TRAINING<br>Warm-up<br>5 minutes<br>on the bike.<br><br>**SUPERSET CIRCUIT**<br>**3 sets x 15 reps each**<br>• Arnolds<br>• Seated Dumbbell Curls<br>• Tricep Rope Pulldowns<br><br>**SUPERSET**<br>**3 sets x 15 reps each**<br>• Cybex® Overhead Press<br>• Cybex® Reverse Fly<br><br>**SUPERSET**<br>**3 sets x 15 reps each**<br>• Cybex® Arm Curl Machine<br>• Tricep Rope Pulldowns<br><br>**SUPERSET CIRCUIT**<br>**2 sets x 20 reps each**<br>• Lower Ab Roll Ups<br>• Upper Ab Roll Ups<br>• Rotary Torso<br><br>10 minutes<br>elliptical machine<br>20 minutes treadmill<br><br>2:00 pm<br>POSTWORKOUT MEAL<br>Eat healthy, high protein with carbs. | Run, hike, or bike<br>45 minutes<br>MODERATE INTENSITY | 11:00 am<br>PREWORKOUT MEAL<br>Eat light, healthy carbs and proteins.<br><br>12:00 pm<br>WEIGHT TRAINING<br>Warm-up<br>5 minutes<br>on the bike.<br><br>**SUPERSET**<br>**2 sets x 15 reps each**<br>• Cybex® Chest Advanced Move<br>• Cybex® Row<br><br>**SUPERSET**<br>**2 sets x 15 reps each**<br>• "Pec-Dec" Chest Fly<br>• Close Grip Front Pulldowns<br><br>**SUPERSET**<br>**2 sets x 15 reps each**<br>• Leg Press<br>• Butt Blaster®<br><br>**SUPERSET CIRCUIT**<br>**2 sets x 15 reps each**<br>• Hip Abduction<br>• Hip Adduction<br>• Seated Leg Curls<br><br>**SUPERSET CIRCUIT**<br>**3 sets x 15 reps each**<br>• Dumbbell Incline Press<br>• Hammer Front Pulldowns<br>• Standing Dumbbell Curls<br><br>**SUPERSET CIRCUIT**<br>**2 sets x 20 reps each**<br>• Lower Ab Roll Ups<br>• Upper Ab Roll Ups<br>• Rotary Torso<br><br>10 minutes<br>elliptical machine<br>20 minutes treadmill<br><br>2:00 pm<br>POSTWORKOUT MEAL<br>Eat healthy, high protein with carbs. | Run, hike, or bike<br>45 minutes<br>MODERATE INTENSITY | Walk or bike<br>45 minutes<br>LOW INTENSITY |

## ADVANCED WEIGHT-LOSS AND TONE PROGRAM SAMPLE 3x a week
### WEEK THREE

| MONDAY | TUESDAY | WEDNESDAY | THURSDAY | FRIDAY | SATURDAY | SUNDAY |
|---|---|---|---|---|---|---|
| **11:00 am** PREWORKOUT MEAL Eat light, healthy carbs and proteins. | | **11:00 am** PREWORKOUT MEAL Eat light, healthy carbs and proteins. | | **11:00 am** PREWORKOUT MEAL Eat light, healthy carbs and proteins. | | |
| **12:00 pm** WEIGHT TRAINING Warm-up 5 minutes on the bike. | | **12:00 pm** WEIGHT TRAINING Warm-up 5 minutes on the bike. | | **12:00 pm** WEIGHT TRAINING Warm-up 5 minutes on the bike. | | |
| **SUPERSET CIRCUIT** **2 sets x 15 reps each** • Cybex® Chest Advanced Move • Cybex® Row • Cybex® Reverse Fly | | **SUPERSET CIRCUIT** **3 sets x 15 reps each** • Arnolds • Seated Dumbbell Curls • Tricep Rope Pulldowns | | **SUPERSET** **2 sets x 15 reps each** • Cybex® Chest Advanced Move • Cybex® Row | | |
| **SUPERSET** **2 sets x 15 reps each** • Hammer Front Pulldowns • Dumbbell Incline Press | | **SUPERSET** **2 sets x 15 reps each** • Rotators • Dumbbell Lateral Raises | | **SUPERSET** **2 sets x 15 reps each** • "Pec-Dec" Chest Fly • Close Grip Front Pulldowns | | |
| **SUPERSET** **2 sets x 15 reps each** • Hip Abduction • Hip Adduction | Spinning, aerobics, or elliptical machine (no longer than 45 minutes) HIGH INTENSITY | **SUPERSET** **2 sets x 15 reps each** • Cybex® Overhead Press • Cybex® Reverse Fly | Run, hike, or bike 45 minutes MODERATE INTENSITY | **SUPERSET** **2 sets x 15 reps each** • Lunges • Leg Press | Run, hike, or bike 45 minutes MODERATE INTENSITY | Walk or bike 45 minutes LOW INTENSITY |
| **SUPERSET CIRCUIT** **3 sets x 15 reps each** • Lunges • Butt Blaster® • Swiss Ball Squats • Seated Leg Curls | | **SUPERSET** **2 sets x 15 reps each** • Cybex® Arm Curl Machine • Tricep Rope Pulldowns | | **SUPERSET CIRCUIT** **2 sets x 15 reps each** • Hip Abduction • Hip Adduction • Seated Leg Curls | | |
| **SUPERSET CIRCUIT** **2 sets x 20 reps each** • Lower Ab Roll Ups • Upper Ab Roll Ups • Rotary Torso | | **SUPERSET CIRCUIT** **2 sets x 20 reps each** • Lower Ab Roll Ups • Upper Ab Roll Ups • Rotary Torso | | **SUPERSET CIRCUIT** **3 sets x 15 reps each** • Dumbbell Incline Press • Wide Grip Front Pulldowns • Standing Dumbbell Curls | | |
| 10 minutes elliptical machine 20 minutes treadmill | | 10 minutes elliptical machine 20 minutes treadmill | | **SUPERSET CIRCUIT** **2 sets x 20 reps each** • Lower Ab Roll Ups • Upper Ab Roll Ups • Rotary Torso | | |
| **2:00 pm** POSTWORKOUT MEAL Eat healthy, high protein with carbs. | | **2:00 pm** POSTWORKOUT MEAL Eat healthy, high protein with carbs. | | 10 minutes elliptical machine 20 minutes treadmill | | |
| | | | | **2:00 pm** POSTWORKOUT MEAL Eat healthy, high protein with carbs. | | |

## ADVANCED WEIGHT-LOSS AND TONE PROGRAM SAMPLE 3x a week
### WEEK FOUR

| MONDAY | TUESDAY | WEDNESDAY | THURSDAY | FRIDAY | SATURDAY | SUNDAY |
|---|---|---|---|---|---|---|
| 11:00 am<br>PREWORKOUT MEAL<br>Eat light, healthy carbs and proteins. | | 11:00 am<br>PREWORKOUT MEAL<br>Eat light, healthy carbs and proteins. | | 11:00 am<br>PREWORKOUT MEAL<br>Eat light, healthy carbs and proteins. | | |
| 12:00 pm<br>WEIGHT TRAINING<br>Warm-up<br>5 minutes<br>on the bike. | | 12:00 pm<br>WEIGHT TRAINING<br>Warm-up<br>5 minutes<br>on the bike. | | 12:00 pm<br>WEIGHT TRAINING<br>Warm-up<br>5 minutes<br>on the bike. | | |
| SUPERSET CIRCUIT<br>2 sets x 15 reps each<br>• Cybex® Chest Advanced Move<br>• Cybex® Row<br>• Cybex® Reverse Fly<br><br>SUPERSET<br>2 sets x 15 reps each<br>• Hammer Front Pulldowns<br>• Dumbbell Incline Press<br><br>SUPERSET<br>2 sets x 15 reps each<br>• Hip Abduction<br>• Hip Adduction<br><br>SUPERSET<br>2 sets x 15 reps each<br>• Leg Extensions<br>• Prone Leg Curls<br><br>SUPERSET CIRCUIT<br>3 sets x 15 reps each<br>• Lunges<br>• Butt Blaster®<br>• Swiss Ball Squats<br><br>SUPERSET CIRCUIT<br>2 sets x 20 reps each<br>• Lower Ab Roll Ups<br>• Upper Ab Roll Ups<br>• Rotary Torso | Spinning, aerobics, or elliptical machine (no longer than 45 minutes)<br>HIGH INTENSITY | SUPERSET CIRCUIT<br>3 sets x 15 reps each<br>• Arnolds<br>• Seated Dumbbell Curls<br>• Tricep Rope Pulldowns<br><br>SUPERSET<br>3 sets x 15 reps each<br>• Cybex® Overhead Press<br>• Cybex® Reverse Fly<br><br>SUPERSET<br>3 sets x 15 reps each<br>• Cybex® Arm Curl Machine<br>• Tricep Rope Pulldowns<br><br>SUPERSET CIRCUIT<br>2 sets x 20 reps each<br>• Lower Ab Roll Ups<br>• Upper Ab Roll Ups<br>• Rotary Torso | Run, hike, or bike 45 minutes<br>MODERATE INTENSITY | SUPERSET<br>2 sets x 15 reps each<br>• Cybex® Chest Advanced Move<br>• Cybex® Row<br><br>SUPERSET<br>2 sets x 15 reps each<br>• "Pec-Dec" Chest Fly<br>• Close Grip Front Pulldowns<br><br>SUPERSET<br>2 sets x 15 reps each<br>• Lunges<br>• Leg Press<br><br>SUPERSET CIRCUIT<br>2 sets x 15 reps each<br>• Hip Abduction<br>• Hip Adduction<br>• Seated Leg Curls<br><br>SUPERSET CIRCUIT<br>3 sets x 15 reps each<br>• Dumbbell Incline Press<br>• Hammer Front Pulldowns<br>• Standing Dumbbell Curls<br><br>SUPERSET CIRCUIT<br>2 sets x 20 reps each<br>• Lower Ab Roll Ups<br>• Upper Ab Roll Ups<br>• Rotary Torso | Run, hike, or bike 45 minutes<br>MODERATE INTENSITY | Walk or bike 45 minutes<br>LOW INTENSITY |
| 10 minutes<br>elliptical machine<br>20 minutes treadmill | | 10 minutes<br>elliptical machine<br>20 minutes treadmill | | 10 minutes<br>elliptical machine<br>20 minutes treadmill | | |
| 2:00 pm<br>POSTWORKOUT MEAL<br>Eat healthy, high protein with carbs. | | 2:00 pm<br>POSTWORKOUT MEAL<br>Eat healthy, high protein with carbs. | | 2:00 pm<br>POSTWORKOUT MEAL<br>Eat healthy, high protein with carbs. | | |

## ADVANCED WEIGHT-LOSS AND TONE PROGRAM SAMPLE 4x a week
WEEK ONE

| MONDAY | TUESDAY | WEDNESDAY | THURSDAY | FRIDAY | SATURDAY | SUNDAY |
|---|---|---|---|---|---|---|
| 11:00 am PREWORKOUT MEAL Eat light, healthy carbs and proteins. | 11:00 am PREWORKOUT MEAL Eat light, healthy carbs and proteins. | | 11:00 am PREWORKOUT MEAL Eat light, healthy carbs and proteins. | 11:00 am PREWORKOUT MEAL Eat light, healthy carbs and proteins. | | |
| 12:00 pm WEIGHT TRAINING Warm-up 5 minutes on the bike. | 12:00 pm WEIGHT TRAINING Warm-up 5 minutes on the bike. | | 12:00 pm WEIGHT TRAINING Warm-up 5 minutes on the bike. | 12:00 pm WEIGHT TRAINING Warm-up 5 minutes on the bike. | | |
| **SUPERSET** **2 sets x 15 reps each** • Hip Abduction • Hip Adduction | **SUPERSET** **2 sets x 15 reps each** • Cybex® Chest Advanced Move • Cybex® Row | | **SUPERSET CIRCUIT** **2 sets x 15 reps each** • Hip Abduction • Hip Adduction • Seated Leg Curls | **SUPERSET CIRCUIT** **3 sets x 15 reps each** • Arnolds • Seated Dumbbell Curls • Tricep Rope Pulldowns | | |
| **SUPERSET CIRCUIT** **2 sets x 15 reps each** • Leg Extensions • Prone Leg Curls • Rotary Calf Machine | **SUPERSET** **2 sets x 15 reps each** • "Pec-Dec" Chest Fly • Close Grip Front Pulldowns | | **SUPERSET CIRCUIT** **2 sets x 15 reps each** • Leg Extensions • Prone Leg Curls • Rotary Calf Machine | **SUPERSET CIRCUIT** **3 sets x 15 reps each** • Dumbbell Incline Press • Wide Grip Front Pulldowns • Standing Dumbbell Curls | | |
| **SUPERSET CIRCUIT** **3 sets x 15 reps each** • Lunges • Butt Blaster® • Leg Press | **SUPERSET** **2 sets x 15 reps each** • Cybex® Overhead Press • Cybex® Reverse Fly | Run, hike, or bike 45 minutes MODERATE INTENSITY | **SUPERSET CIRCUIT** **3 sets x 15 reps each** • Lunges • Butt Blaster® • Leg Press | **SUPERSET** **2 sets x 15 reps each** • Rotators • Dumbbell Lateral Raises | Run, hike, or bike 45 minutes MODERATE INTENSITY | Walk or bike 45 minutes LOW INTENSITY |
| **SUPERSET CIRCUIT** **2 sets x 20 reps each** • Lower Ab Roll Ups • Upper Ab Roll Ups • Rotary Torso | **SUPERSET** **2 sets x 15 reps each** • Cybex® Arm Curl Machine • Tricep Rope Pulldowns | | **SUPERSET CIRCUIT** **2 sets x 20 reps each** • Lower Ab Roll Ups • Upper Ab Roll Ups • Rotary Torso | **SUPERSET CIRCUIT** **2 sets x 20 reps each** • Lower Back Hyperextensions • Lower Ab Roll Ups • Upper Ab Roll Ups • Rotary Torso | | |
| 10 minutes elliptical machine 20 minutes treadmill | **SUPERSET** **3 sets x 15 reps each** • Dumbbell Incline Press • Wide Grip Front Pulldowns | | 10 minutes elliptical machine 20 minutes treadmill | 10 minutes elliptical machine 20 minutes treadmill | | |
| 2:00 pm POSTWORKOUT MEAL Eat healthy, high protein with carbs. | **SUPERSET CIRCUIT** **2 sets x 20 reps each** • Lower Back Hyperextensions • Lower Ab Roll Ups • Upper Ab Roll Ups • Rotary Torso | | 2:00 pm POSTWORKOUT MEAL Eat healthy, high protein with carbs. | 2:00 pm POSTWORKOUT MEAL Eat healthy, high protein with carbs. | | |
| | 10 minutes elliptical machine 20 minutes treadmill | | | | | |
| | 2:00 pm POSTWORKOUT MEAL Eat healthy, high protein with carbs. | | | | | |

## ADVANCED WEIGHT-LOSS AND TONE PROGRAM SAMPLE 4x a week
### WEEK TWO

| MONDAY | TUESDAY | WEDNESDAY | THURSDAY | FRIDAY | SATURDAY | SUNDAY |
|---|---|---|---|---|---|---|
| 11:00 am<br>PREWORKOUT MEAL<br>Eat light, healthy carbs and proteins. | 11:00 am<br>PREWORKOUT MEAL<br>Eat light, healthy carbs and proteins. | | 11:00 am<br>PREWORKOUT MEAL<br>Eat light, healthy carbs and proteins. | 11:00 am<br>PREWORKOUT MEAL<br>Eat light, healthy carbs and proteins. | | |
| 12:00 pm<br>WEIGHT TRAINING<br>Warm-up<br>5 minutes<br>on the bike. | 12:00 pm<br>WEIGHT TRAINING<br>Warm-up<br>5 minutes<br>on the bike. | | 12:00 pm<br>WEIGHT TRAINING<br>Warm-up<br>5 minutes<br>on the bike. | 12:00 pm<br>WEIGHT TRAINING<br>Warm-up<br>5 minutes<br>on the bike. | | |
| **SUPERSET CIRCUIT**<br>**3 sets x 15 reps each**<br>• Hip Abduction<br>• Hip Adduction<br>• Lunges<br>• Butt Blaster®<br>• Swiss Ball Squats<br>• Lower Ab Roll Ups | **SUPERSET**<br>**3 sets x 15 reps each**<br>• Cybex® Chest Advanced Move<br>• Cybex® Row<br><br>**SUPERSET**<br>**3 sets x 15 reps each**<br>• "Pec-Dec" Chest Fly<br>• Close Grip Front Pulldowns | | **SUPERSET CIRCUIT**<br>**3 sets x 15 reps each**<br>• Hip Abduction<br>• Hip Adduction<br>• Lunges<br>• Butt Blaster®<br>• Swiss Ball Squats<br>• Lower Ab Roll Ups | **SUPERSET CIRCUIT**<br>**3 sets x 15 reps each**<br>• Arnolds<br>• Seated Dumbbell Curls<br>• Tricep Rope Pulldowns | Run, hike, or bike<br>45 minutes<br>MODERATE INTENSITY | Walk or bike<br>45 minutes<br>LOW INTENSITY |
| 10 minutes<br>elliptical machine<br>20 minutes treadmill | **SUPERSET**<br>**3 sets x 15 reps each**<br>• Cybex® Overhead Press<br>• Cybex® Reverse Fly | Run, hike, or bike<br>45 minutes<br>MODERATE INTENSITY | 10 minutes<br>elliptical machine<br>20 minutes treadmill | **SUPERSET CIRCUIT**<br>**3 sets x 15 reps each**<br>• Dumbbell Incline Press<br>• Wide Grip Front Pulldowns<br>• Standing Dumbbell Curls | | |
| 2:00 pm<br>POSTWORKOUT MEAL<br>Eat healthy, high protein with carbs. | **SUPERSET**<br>**3 sets x 15 reps each**<br>• Cybex® Arm Curl Machine<br>• Tricep Rope Pulldowns | | 2:00 pm<br>POSTWORKOUT MEAL<br>Eat healthy, high protein with carbs. | **SUPERSET**<br>**2 sets x 15 reps each**<br>• Cybex® Overhead Press<br>• Cybex® Reverse Fly | | |
| | **SUPERSET**<br>**3 sets x 15 reps each**<br>• Dumbbell Incline Press<br>• Wide Grip Front Pulldowns | | | **SUPERSET CIRCUIT**<br>**2 sets x 20 reps each**<br>• Lower Back Hyperextensions<br>• Lower Ab Roll Ups<br>• Upper Ab Roll Ups<br>• Rotary Torso | | |
| | **SUPERSET CIRCUIT**<br>**2 sets x 20 reps each**<br>• Lower Back Hyperextensions<br>• Lower Ab Roll Ups<br>• Upper Ab Roll Ups<br>• Rotary Torso | | | 10 minutes<br>elliptical machine<br>20 minutes treadmill | | |
| | 10 minutes<br>elliptical machine<br>20 minutes treadmill | | | 2:00 pm<br>POSTWORKOUT MEAL<br>Eat healthy, high protein with carbs. | | |
| | 2:00 pm<br>POSTWORKOUT MEAL<br>Eat healthy, high protein with carbs. | | | | | |

## ADVANCED WEIGHT-LOSS AND TONE PROGRAM SAMPLE 4x a week
### WEEK THREE

| MONDAY | TUESDAY | WEDNESDAY | THURSDAY | FRIDAY | SATURDAY | SUNDAY |
|---|---|---|---|---|---|---|
| 11:00 am<br>PREWORKOUT MEAL<br>Eat light, healthy carbs and proteins. | 11:00 am<br>PREWORKOUT MEAL<br>Eat light, healthy carbs and proteins. | | 11:00 am<br>PREWORKOUT MEAL<br>Eat light, healthy carbs and proteins. | 11:00 am<br>PREWORKOUT MEAL<br>Eat light, healthy carbs and proteins. | | |
| 12:00 pm<br>WEIGHT TRAINING<br>Warm-up<br>5 minutes<br>on the bike. | 12:00 pm<br>WEIGHT TRAINING<br>Warm-up<br>5 minutes<br>on the bike. | | 12:00 pm<br>WEIGHT TRAINING<br>Warm-up<br>5 minutes<br>on the bike. | 12:00 pm<br>WEIGHT TRAINING<br>Warm-up<br>5 minutes<br>on the bike. | | |
| **SUPERSET**<br>**2 sets x 15 reps each**<br>• Hip Abduction<br>• Hip Adduction<br><br>**SUPERSET CIRCUIT**<br>**2 sets x 15 reps each**<br>• Leg Extensions<br>• Prone Leg Curls<br>• Rotary Calf Machine<br><br>**SUPERSET CIRCUIT**<br>**3 sets x 15 reps each**<br>• Lunges<br>• Butt Blaster®<br>• Leg Press<br><br>**SUPERSET CIRCUIT**<br>**2 sets x 20 reps each**<br>• Lower Ab Roll Ups<br>• Upper Ab Roll Ups<br>• Rotary Torso<br><br>10 minutes<br>elliptical machine<br>20 minutes treadmill<br><br>2:00 pm<br>POSTWORKOUT MEAL<br>Eat healthy, high protein with carbs. | **SUPERSET**<br>**2 sets x 15 reps each**<br>• Cybex® Chest Advanced Move<br>• Cybex® Row<br><br>**SUPERSET**<br>**2 sets x 15 reps each**<br>• "Pec-Dec" Chest Fly<br>• Close Grip Front Pulldowns<br><br>**SUPERSET**<br>**2 sets x 15 reps each**<br>• Cybex® Overhead Press<br>• Cybex® Reverse Fly<br><br>**SUPERSET**<br>**2 sets x 15 reps each**<br>• Cybex® Arm Curl Machine<br>• Tricep Rope Pulldowns<br><br>**SUPERSET**<br>**3 sets x 15 reps each**<br>• Dumbbell Incline Press<br>• Wide Grip Front Pulldowns<br><br>**SUPERSET CIRCUIT**<br>**2 sets x 20 reps each**<br>• Lower Back Hyperextensions<br>• Lower Ab Roll Ups<br>• Upper Ab Roll Ups<br>• Rotary Torso<br><br>10 minutes<br>elliptical machine<br>20 minutes treadmill<br><br>2:00 pm<br>POSTWORKOUT MEAL<br>Eat healthy, high protein with carbs. | Run, hike, or bike<br>45 minutes<br>MODERATE INTENSITY | **SUPERSET CIRCUIT**<br>**2 sets x 15 reps each**<br>• Hip Abduction<br>• Hip Adduction<br>• Seated Leg Curls<br><br>**SUPERSET CIRCUIT**<br>**2 sets x 15 reps each**<br>• Leg Extensions<br>• Prone Leg Curls<br>• Rotary Calf Machine<br><br>**SUPERSET CIRCUIT**<br>**3 sets x 15 reps each**<br>• Lunges<br>• Butt Blaster®<br>• Leg Press<br><br>**SUPERSET CIRCUIT**<br>**2 sets x 20 reps each**<br>• Lower Ab Roll Ups<br>• Upper Ab Roll Ups<br>• Rotary Torso<br><br>10 minutes<br>elliptical machine<br>20 minutes treadmill<br><br>2:00 pm<br>POSTWORKOUT MEAL<br>Eat healthy, high protein with carbs. | **SUPERSET CIRCUIT**<br>**3 sets x 15 reps each**<br>• Arnolds<br>• Seated Dumbbell Curls<br>• Tricep Rope Pulldowns<br><br>**SUPERSET CIRCUIT**<br>**3 sets x 15 reps each**<br>• Dumbbell Incline Press<br>• Wide Grip Front Pulldowns<br>• Standing Dumbbell Curls<br><br>**SUPERSET**<br>**2 sets x 15 reps each**<br>• Rotators<br>• Dumbbell Lateral Raises<br><br>**SUPERSET CIRCUIT**<br>**2 sets x 20 reps each**<br>• Lower Back Hyperextensions<br>• Lower Ab Roll Ups<br>• Upper Ab Roll Ups<br>• Rotary Torso<br><br>10 minutes<br>elliptical machine<br>20 minutes treadmill<br><br>2:00 pm<br>POSTWORKOUT MEAL<br>Eat healthy, high protein with carbs. | Run, hike, or bike<br>45 minutes<br>MODERATE INTENSITY | Walk or bike<br>45 minutes<br>LOW INTENSITY |

## ADVANCED WEIGHT-LOSS AND TONE PROGRAM SAMPLE 4x a week
### WEEK FOUR

| MONDAY | TUESDAY | WEDNESDAY | THURSDAY | FRIDAY | SATURDAY | SUNDAY |
|---|---|---|---|---|---|---|
| 11:00 am<br>PREWORKOUT MEAL<br>Eat light, healthy carbs and proteins. | 11:00 am<br>PREWORKOUT MEAL<br>Eat light, healthy carbs and proteins. | | 11:00 am<br>PREWORKOUT MEAL<br>Eat light, healthy carbs and proteins. | 11:00 am<br>PREWORKOUT MEAL<br>Eat light, healthy carbs and proteins. | | |
| 12:00 pm<br>WEIGHT TRAINING<br>Warm-up<br>5 minutes<br>on the bike. | 12:00 pm<br>WEIGHT TRAINING<br>Warm-up<br>5 minutes<br>on the bike. | | 12:00 pm<br>WEIGHT TRAINING<br>Warm-up<br>5 minutes<br>on the bike. | 12:00 pm<br>WEIGHT TRAINING<br>Warm-up<br>5 minutes<br>on the bike. | | |
| **SUPERSET CIRCUIT**<br>**3 sets x 15 reps each**<br>• Hip Abduction<br>• Hip Adduction<br>• Lunges<br>• Butt Blaster®<br>• Swiss Ball Squats<br>• Lower Ab Roll Ups<br><br>10 minutes elliptical machine 20 minutes treadmill<br><br>2:00 pm<br>POSTWORKOUT MEAL<br>Eat healthy, high protein with carbs. | **SUPERSET**<br>**2 sets x 15 reps each**<br>• Cybex® Chest Advanced Move<br>• Cybex® Row<br><br>**SUPERSET**<br>**2 sets x 15 reps each**<br>• "Pec-Dec" Chest Fly<br>• Close Grip Front Pulldowns<br><br>**SUPERSET**<br>**2 sets x 15 reps each**<br>• Cybex® Overhead Press<br>• Cybex® Reverse Fly<br><br>**SUPERSET**<br>**2 sets x 15 reps each**<br>• Cybex® Arm Curl Machine<br>• Tricep Rope Pulldowns<br><br>**SUPERSET**<br>**3 sets x 15 reps each**<br>• Dumbbell Incline Press<br>• Wide Grip Front Pulldowns<br><br>**SUPERSET CIRCUIT**<br>**2 sets x 20 reps each**<br>• Lower Back Hyperextensions<br>• Lower Ab Roll Ups<br>• Upper Ab Roll Ups<br>• Rotary Torso<br><br>10 minutes elliptical machine 20 minutes treadmill<br><br>2:00 pm<br>POSTWORKOUT MEAL<br>Eat healthy, high protein with carbs. | Run, hike, or bike<br>45 minutes<br>MODERATE INTENSITY | **SUPERSET CIRCUIT**<br>**3 sets x 15 reps each**<br>• Hip Abduction<br>• Hip Adduction<br>• Lunges<br>• Butt Blaster®<br>• Swiss Ball Squats<br>• Lower Ab Roll Ups<br><br>10 minutes elliptical machine 20 minutes treadmill<br><br>2:00 pm<br>POSTWORKOUT MEAL<br>Eat healthy, high protein with carbs. | **SUPERSET CIRCUIT**<br>**3 sets x 15 reps each**<br>• Arnolds<br>• Seated Dumbbell Curls<br>• Tricep Rope Pulldowns<br><br>**SUPERSET CIRCUIT**<br>**3 sets x 15 reps each**<br>• Dumbbell Incline Press<br>• Wide Grip Front Pulldowns<br>• Standing Dumbbell Curls<br><br>**SUPERSET**<br>**2 sets x 15 reps each**<br>• Cybex® Overhead Press<br>• Cybex® Reverse Fly<br><br>**SUPERSET CIRCUIT**<br>**2 sets x 20 reps each**<br>• Lower Back Hyperextensions<br>• Lower Ab Roll Ups<br>• Upper Ab Roll Ups<br>• Rotary Torso<br><br>10 minutes elliptical machine 20 minutes treadmill<br><br>2:00 pm<br>POSTWORKOUT MEAL<br>Eat healthy, high protein with carbs. | Run, hike, or bike<br>45 minutes<br>MODERATE INTENSITY | Walk or bike<br>45 minutes<br>LOW INTENSITY |

# the advanced power and strength programs

This program is designed for anyone who wants to increase strength and power while minimizing the risk of injury. Additional benefits of this program are to produce muscle symmetry and balance. This approach utilizes a lower number of repetitions (6 to 10) and multiple BAM Supersets targeting specific areas. It is important to note that this is an advanced program designed for experienced, healthy weight lifters.

A common myth is that your goals will be met more quickly by increasing the length of workouts and the number of sets. In reality, this leads to overtraining and constant muscle tissue breakdown. For optimal results and recovery, it is important to keep your weight training workouts to less than an hour.

The cardio program should be done daily, but at low to moderate intensity. Cardio training at a high intensity is counterproductive because it hinders adequate recovery, resulting in overtraining.

A healthy and balanced diet is also critical to power and strength programs. Due to the increased resistance loads and resulting muscle tissue breakdown, it is extremely important to provide the body with an adequate and nutritious source of protein. Therefore, the pre- and postworkout meals are extremely important.

In the four-week workout layouts below, we have included samples for strength training at a frequency of two, three, and four times a week. Working out two times a week will typically allow you to maintain current levels of strength and muscle tone. Working out three times a week will allow you to improve current levels and achieve their personal goals more readily. A four times a week schedule is for if you are seeking more strength, muscle mass, and overall definition.

| key points | CONSISTENCY, CORRECT TECHNIQUE, LOWER REPETITIONS WITH INCREASED WEIGHT AND NUMBER OF SETS, DAILY CARDIO AT LOW- TO MODERATE-INTENSITY LEVELS, AND QUALITY NUTRITION WITH AN EMPHASIS ON QUALITY PROTEIN. |
|---|---|

**ADVANCED POWER AND STRENGTH PROGRAM SAMPLE 2x a week**
WEEK ONE

| MONDAY | TUESDAY | WEDNESDAY | THURSDAY | FRIDAY | SATURDAY | SUNDAY |
|---|---|---|---|---|---|---|
| 11:00 am<br>PREWORKOUT MEAL<br>Eat light, healthy carbs and proteins.<br><br>12:00 pm<br>WEIGHT TRAINING<br>Warm-up<br>5 minutes<br>on the bike.<br><br>**SUPERSET CIRCUIT**<br>**4 sets x 8 reps each**<br>• Bench Press<br>• Front Pulldowns<br>• Standing Dumbbell Curls<br><br>**SUPERSET**<br>**3 sets x 8 reps each**<br>• Hammer Front Pulldowns<br>• Dumbbell Incline Press<br><br>**SUPERSET CIRCUIT**<br>**4 sets x 10 reps each**<br>• Leg Extensions<br>• Prone Leg Curls<br>• Rotary Calf Machine<br><br>**SUPERSET**<br>**3 sets x 15 reps each**<br>• Lower Ab Roll Ups<br>• Upper Ab Roll Ups<br><br>10 minutes elliptical machine 20 minutes treadmill<br><br>2:00 pm<br>POSTWORKOUT MEAL<br>Eat healthy, high protein with carbs. | Spinning, aerobics, or elliptical machine (no longer than 45 minutes)<br>MODERATE INTENSITY | Walk or bike 45 minutes<br>LOW INTENSITY | 11:00 am<br>PREWORKOUT MEAL<br>Eat light, healthy carbs and proteins.<br><br>12:00 pm<br>WEIGHT TRAINING<br>Warm-up<br>5 minutes<br>on the bike.<br><br>**SUPERSET CIRCUIT**<br>**3 sets x 10 reps each**<br>• Cybex® Chest Advanced Move<br>• Cybex® Row<br>• Cybex® Reverse Fly<br><br>**SUPERSET CIRCUIT**<br>**4 sets x 10 reps each**<br>• Arnolds<br>• Seated Dumbbell Curls<br>• Tricep Rope Pulldowns<br><br>**SUPERSET CIRCUIT**<br>**4 sets x 8 reps each**<br>• Lunges<br>• Butt Blaster®<br>• Leg Press<br>• Seated Leg Curls<br><br>**SUPERSET CIRCUIT**<br>**2 sets x 20 reps each**<br>• Lower Ab Roll Ups<br>• Upper Ab Roll Ups<br>• Rotary Torso<br><br>10 minutes elliptical machine 20 minutes treadmill<br><br>2:00 pm<br>POSTWORKOUT MEAL<br>Eat healthy, high protein with carbs. | Spinning, aerobics, or elliptical machine (no longer than 45 minutes)<br>MODERATE INTENSITY | Walk or bike 45 minutes<br>LOW INTENSITY | Walk 30 minutes<br>LOW INTENSITY |

## ADVANCED POWER AND STRENGTH PROGRAM SAMPLE 2x a week
WEEK TWO

| MONDAY | TUESDAY | WEDNESDAY | THURSDAY | FRIDAY | SATURDAY | SUNDAY |
|---|---|---|---|---|---|---|
| 11:00 am<br>PREWORKOUT MEAL<br>Eat light, healthy carbs and proteins. | | | 11:00 am<br>PREWORKOUT MEAL<br>Eat light, healthy carbs and proteins. | | | |
| 12:00 pm<br>WEIGHT TRAINING<br>Warm-up<br>5 minutes<br>on the bike. | | | 12:00 pm<br>WEIGHT TRAINING<br>Warm-up<br>5 minutes<br>on the bike. | | | |
| **SUPERSET CIRCUIT**<br>**2 sets x 8 reps each**<br>• Incline Bench Press<br>• Close Grip Front Pulldowns<br>• Standing Dumbbell Curls<br><br>**SUPERSET**<br>**3 sets x 8 reps each**<br>• Hammer Front Pulldowns<br>• Dumbbell Incline Press<br><br>**SUPERSET**<br>**4 sets x 8 reps each**<br>• Smith Machine Squats<br>• Lunges<br><br>**SOLO EXERCISE**<br>**4 sets x 15 reps**<br>• Rotary Calf Machine<br><br>**SUPERSET CIRCUIT**<br>**2 sets x 20 reps each**<br>• Lower Ab Roll Ups<br>• Upper Ab Roll Ups<br>• Rotary Torso | Spinning, aerobics, or elliptical machine (no longer than 45 minutes)<br>MODERATE INTENSITY | Walk or bike<br>45 minutes<br>LOW INTENSITY | **SUPERSET**<br>**4 sets x 10 reps each**<br>• Cable Crossover<br>• Wide Grip Front Pulldowns<br><br>**SUPERSET**<br>**4 sets x 10 reps each**<br>• Cybex® Overhead Press<br>• Cybex® Reverse Fly<br><br>**SUPERSET**<br>**4 sets x 10 reps each**<br>• Standing Dumbbell Curls<br>• Tricep Rope Pulldowns<br><br>**SUPERSET CIRCUIT**<br>**3 sets x 10 reps each**<br>• Leg Press<br>• Leg Extensions<br>• Seated Leg Curls<br>• Swiss Ball Squats<br><br>**SUPERSET CIRCUIT**<br>**2 sets x 20 reps each**<br>• Lower Ab Roll Ups<br>• Upper Ab Roll Ups<br>• Rotary Torso | Spinning, aerobics, or elliptical machine (no longer than 45 minutes)<br>MODERATE INTENSITY | Walk or bike<br>45 minutes<br>LOW INTENSITY | Walk 30 minutes<br>LOW INTENSITY |
| 20 minutes treadmill | | | 20 minutes treadmill | | | |
| 2:00 pm<br>POSTWORKOUT MEAL<br>Eat healthy, high protein with carbs. | | | 2:00 pm<br>POSTWORKOUT MEAL<br>Eat healthy, high protein with carbs. | | | |

## ADVANCED POWER AND STRENGTH PROGRAM SAMPLE 2x a week
### WEEK THREE

| MONDAY | TUESDAY | WEDNESDAY | THURSDAY | FRIDAY | SATURDAY | SUNDAY |
|---|---|---|---|---|---|---|
| 11:00 am<br>PREWORKOUT MEAL<br>Eat light, healthy carbs and proteins.<br><br>12:00 pm<br>WEIGHT TRAINING<br>Warm-up<br>5 minutes<br>on the bike.<br><br>**SUPERSET CIRCUIT**<br>**5 sets x 7 reps each**<br>• Bench Press<br>• Front Pulldowns<br>• Standing Dumbbell Curls<br><br>**SUPERSET**<br>**2 sets x 10 reps each**<br>• Hammer Front Pulldowns<br>• Dumbbell Incline Press<br><br>**SUPERSET**<br>**4 sets x 8 reps each**<br>• Smith Machine Squats<br>• Lunges<br><br>**SUPERSET**<br>**3 sets x 8 reps each**<br>• Lower Ab Roll Ups<br>• Upper Ab Roll Ups<br><br>20 minutes treadmill<br><br>2:00 pm<br>POSTWORKOUT MEAL<br>Eat healthy, high protein with carbs. | Spinning, aerobics, or elliptical machine (no longer than 45 minutes)<br>MODERATE INTENSITY | Walk or bike 45 minutes<br>LOW INTENSITY | 11:00 am<br>PREWORKOUT MEAL<br>Eat light, healthy carbs and proteins.<br><br>12:00 pm<br>WEIGHT TRAINING<br>Warm-up<br>5 minutes<br>on the bike.<br><br>**SUPERSET CIRCUIT**<br>**4 sets x 8 reps each**<br>• Cybex® Chest Advanced Move<br>• Cybex® Row<br>• Cybex® Reverse Fly<br><br>**SUPERSET CIRCUIT**<br>**4 sets x 10 reps each**<br>• Arnolds<br>• Seated Dumbbell Curls<br>• Tricep Rope Pulldowns<br><br>**SUPERSET CIRCUIT**<br>**4 sets x 8 reps each**<br>• Leg Press<br>• Leg Extensions<br>• Seated Leg Curls<br><br>**SOLO EXERCISE**<br>**4 sets x 15 reps**<br>• Rotary Calf Machine<br><br>**SUPERSET CIRCUIT**<br>**2 sets x 20 reps each**<br>• Lower Ab Roll Ups<br>• Upper Ab Roll Ups<br>• Rotary Torso<br><br>20 minutes treadmill<br><br>2:00 pm<br>POSTWORKOUT MEAL<br>Eat healthy, high protein with carbs. | Spinning, aerobics, or elliptical machine (no longer than 45 minutes)<br>MODERATE INTENSITY | Walk or bike 45 minutes<br>LOW INTENSITY | Walk 30 minutes<br>LOW INTENSITY |

## ADVANCED POWER AND STRENGTH PROGRAM SAMPLE 2x a week
WEEK FOUR

| MONDAY | TUESDAY | WEDNESDAY | THURSDAY | FRIDAY | SATURDAY | SUNDAY |
|---|---|---|---|---|---|---|
| 11:00 am<br>PREWORKOUT MEAL<br>Eat light, healthy carbs and proteins. | | | 11:00 pm<br>PREWORKOUT MEAL<br>Eat light, healthy carbs and proteins. | | | |
| 12:00 pm<br>WEIGHT TRAINING<br>Warm-up<br>5 minutes<br>on the bike. | | | 12:00 pm<br>WEIGHT TRAINING<br>Warm-up<br>5 minutes<br>on the bike. | | | |
| **SUPERSET CIRCUIT**<br>**5 sets x 7 reps each**<br>• Incline Bench Press<br>• Close Grip Front Pulldowns<br>• Standing Dumbbell Curls<br><br>**SUPERSET**<br>**2 sets x 10 reps each**<br>• Hammer Front Pulldowns<br>• Dumbbell Incline Press<br><br>**SUPERSET CIRCUIT**<br>**4 sets x 8 reps each**<br>• Leg Press<br>• Leg Extensions<br>• Seated Leg Curls<br><br>**SOLO EXERCISE**<br>**4 sets x 15 reps**<br>• Rotary Calf Machine<br><br>**SUPERSET CIRCUIT**<br>**2 sets x 20 reps each**<br>• Lower Ab Roll Ups<br>• Upper Ab Roll Ups<br>• Rotary Torso | Spinning, aerobics, or elliptical machine (no longer than 45 minutes)<br>MODERATE INTENSITY | Walk or bike<br>45 minutes<br>LOW INTENSITY | **SUPERSET**<br>**4 sets x 10 reps each**<br>• "Pec-Dec" Chest Fly<br>• "Pec-Dec" Reverse Fly<br><br>**SUPERSET**<br>**3 sets x 10 reps each**<br>• Cybex® Overhead Press<br>• Cybex® Reverse Fly<br><br>**SUPERSET CIRCUIT**<br>**3 sets x 10 reps each**<br>• Arnolds<br>• Standing Dumbbell Curls<br>• Tricep Rope Pulldowns<br><br>**SUPERSET**<br>**4 sets x 10 reps each**<br>• Smith Machine Squats<br>• Lunges<br><br>**SUPERSET CIRCUIT**<br>**2 sets x 20 reps each**<br>• Lower Ab Roll Ups<br>• Upper Ab Roll Ups<br>• Rotary Torso | Spinning, aerobics, or elliptical machine (no longer than 45 minutes)<br>MODERATE INTENSITY | Walk or bike<br>45 minutes<br>LOW INTENSITY | Walk 30 minutes<br>LOW INTENSITY |
| 20 minutes treadmill | | | 20 minutes treadmill | | | |
| 2:00 pm<br>POSTWORKOUT MEAL<br>Eat healthy, high protein with carbs. | | | 2:00 pm<br>POSTWORKOUT MEAL<br>Eat healthy, high protein with carbs. | | | |

## ADVANCED POWER AND STRENGTH PROGRAM SAMPLE 3x a week
### WEEK ONE

| MONDAY | TUESDAY | WEDNESDAY | THURSDAY | FRIDAY | SATURDAY | SUNDAY |
|---|---|---|---|---|---|---|
| 11:00 am<br>PREWORKOUT MEAL<br>Eat light, healthy carbs and proteins. | | 11:00 am<br>PREWORKOUT MEAL<br>Eat light, healthy carbs and proteins. | | 11:00 am<br>PREWORKOUT MEAL<br>Eat light, healthy carbs and proteins. | | |
| 12:00 pm<br>WEIGHT TRAINING<br>Warm-up<br>5 minutes<br>on the bike. | | 12:00 pm<br>WEIGHT TRAINING<br>Warm-up<br>5 minutes<br>on the bike. | | 12:00 pm<br>WEIGHT TRAINING<br>Warm-up<br>5 minutes<br>on the bike. | | |
| SUPERSET CIRCUIT<br>4 sets x 8 reps each<br>• Bench Press<br>• Hammer Front Pulldowns<br>• Standing Dumbbell Curls<br><br>SUPERSET CIRCUIT<br>4 sets x 8 reps each<br>• Lunges<br>• Leg Press<br>• Seated Leg Curls<br><br>SUPERSET<br>3 sets x 8 reps each<br>• Wide Grip Front Pulldowns<br>• Dumbbell Incline Press<br><br>SOLO EXERCISE<br>4 sets x 8 reps<br>• Rotary Calf Machine<br><br>SUPERSET<br>2 sets x 20 reps each<br>• Lower Ab Roll Ups<br>• Upper Ab Roll Ups<br><br>20 minutes treadmill | Spinning, aerobics, or elliptical machine (no longer than 45 minutes)<br><br>MODERATE INTENSITY | SUPERSET CIRCUIT<br>3 sets x 8 reps each<br>• Arnolds<br>• Seated Dumbbell Curls<br>• Tricep Rope Pulldowns<br><br>SUPERSET<br>2 sets x 12 reps each<br>• Rotators<br>• Dumbbell Lateral Raises<br><br>SUPERSET<br>3 sets x 10 reps each<br>• Cybex® Overhead Press<br>• Cybex® Reverse Fly<br><br>SUPERSET<br>3 sets x 10 reps each<br>• Standing Barbell Curls<br>• Tricep Rope Pulldowns<br><br>SUPERSET CIRCUIT<br>2 sets x 20 reps each<br>• Lower Ab Roll Ups<br>• Upper Ab Roll Ups<br>• Rotary Torso<br><br>20 minutes treadmill | Run, hike, or bike<br>45 minutes<br>MODERATE INTENSITY | SUPERSET CIRCUIT<br>3 sets x 8 reps each<br>• Cybex® Chest Advanced Move<br>• Cybex® Row<br>• Cybex® Reverse Box<br><br>SUPERSET<br>3 sets x 8 reps each<br>• "Pec-Dec" Chest Fly<br>• Close Grip Front Pulldowns<br><br>SUPERSET CIRCUIT<br>4 sets x 8 reps each<br>• Smith Machine Squats<br>• Leg Press<br>• Butt Blaster®<br><br>SUPERSET<br>3 sets x 10 reps each<br>• Leg Extensions<br>• Seated Leg Curls<br><br>SUPERSET CIRCUIT<br>2 sets x 20 reps each<br>• Lower Ab Roll Ups<br>• Upper Ab Roll Ups<br>• Rotary Torso<br><br>20 minutes treadmill | Run, hike, or bike<br>45 minutes<br>MODERATE INTENSITY | Walk or bike<br>45 minutes<br>LOW INTENSITY |
| 2:00 pm<br>POSTWORKOUT MEAL<br>Eat healthy, high protein with carbs. | | 2:00 pm<br>POSTWORKOUT MEAL<br>Eat healthy, high protein with carbs. | | 2:00 pm<br>POSTWORKOUT MEAL<br>Eat healthy, high protein with carbs. | | |

## ADVANCED POWER AND STRENGTH PROGRAM SAMPLE 3x a week
WEEK TWO

| MONDAY | TUESDAY | WEDNESDAY | THURSDAY | FRIDAY | SATURDAY | SUNDAY |
|---|---|---|---|---|---|---|
| 11:00 am<br>PREWORKOUT MEAL<br>Eat light, healthy carbs and proteins. | | 11:00 am<br>PREWORKOUT MEAL<br>Eat light, healthy carbs and proteins. | | 11:00 am<br>PREWORKOUT MEAL<br>Eat light, healthy carbs and proteins. | | |
| 12:00 pm<br>WEIGHT TRAINING<br>Warm-up<br>5 minutes<br>on the bike. | | 12:00 pm<br>WEIGHT TRAINING<br>Warm-up<br>5 minutes<br>on the bike. | | 12:00 pm<br>WEIGHT TRAINING<br>Warm-up<br>5 minutes<br>on the bike. | | |
| **SUPERSET CIRCUIT**<br>**4 sets x 8 reps each**<br>• Incline Bench Press<br>• Wide Grip Front Pulldowns<br>• Standing Barbell Curls | | **SUPERSET CIRCUIT**<br>**4 sets x 8 reps each**<br>• Arnolds<br>• Seated Dumbbell Curls<br>• Tricep Rope Pulldowns | | **SUPERSET CIRCUIT**<br>**3 sets x 8 reps each**<br>• Cybex® Chest Advanced Move<br>• Cybex® Row<br>• Cybex® Reverse Box | | |
| **SUPERSET CIRCUIT**<br>**4 sets x 8 reps each**<br>• Lunges<br>• Smith Machine Squats<br>• Seated Leg Curls | Spinning, aerobics, or elliptical machine (no longer than 45 minutes)<br>MODERATE INTENSITY | **SUPERSET**<br>**4 sets x 10 reps each**<br>• Cybex® Overhead Press<br>• Cybex® Reverse Fly | Run, hike, or bike<br>45 minutes<br>MODERATE INTENSITY | **SUPERSET**<br>**3 sets x 8 reps each**<br>• Cable Cross-Over Chest Fly<br>• Close Grip Front Pulldowns | Run, hike, or bike<br>45 minutes<br>MODERATE INTENSITY | Walk or bike<br>45 minutes<br>LOW INTENSITY |
| **SUPERSET**<br>**3 sets x 8 reps each**<br>• Hammer Front Pulldowns<br>• Dumbbell Incline Press | | **SUPERSET**<br>**3 sets x 10 reps each**<br>• Standing Hammer Curls<br>• Tricep Rope Pulldowns | | **SUPERSET CIRCUIT**<br>**4 sets x 8 reps each**<br>• Leg Press<br>• Lunges<br>• Leg Extensions<br>• Butt Blaster® | | |
| **SOLO EXERCISE**<br>**4 sets x 15 reps**<br>• Rotary Calf Machine | | **SUPERSET CIRCUIT**<br>**2 sets x 20 reps each**<br>• Lower Ab Roll Ups<br>• Upper Ab Roll Ups<br>• Rotary Torso | | **SUPERSET CIRCUIT**<br>**2 sets x 20 reps each**<br>• Lower Ab Roll Ups<br>• Upper Ab Roll Ups<br>• Rotary Torso | | |
| **SUPERSET**<br>**2 sets x 20 reps each**<br>• Lower Ab Roll Ups<br>• Upper Ab Roll Ups | | 20 minutes treadmill | | 20 minutes treadmill | | |
| 20 minutes treadmill | | 2:00 pm<br>POSTWORKOUT MEAL<br>Eat healthy, high protein with carbs. | | 2:00 pm<br>POSTWORKOUT MEAL<br>Eat healthy, high protein with carbs. | | |
| 2:00 pm<br>POSTWORKOUT MEAL<br>Eat healthy, high protein with carbs. | | | | | | |

## ADVANCED POWER AND STRENGTH PROGRAM SAMPLE 3x a week
### WEEK THREE

| MONDAY | TUESDAY | WEDNESDAY | THURSDAY | FRIDAY | SATURDAY | SUNDAY |
|---|---|---|---|---|---|---|
| 11:00 am<br>PREWORKOUT MEAL<br>Eat light, healthy carbs and proteins. | | 11:00 am<br>PREWORKOUT MEAL<br>Eat light, healthy carbs and proteins. | | 11:00 am<br>PREWORKOUT MEAL<br>Eat light, healthy carbs and proteins. | | |
| 12:00 pm<br>WEIGHT TRAINING<br>Warm-up<br>5 minutes<br>on the bike. | | 12:00 pm<br>WEIGHT TRAINING<br>Warm-up<br>5 minutes<br>on the bike. | | 12:00 pm<br>WEIGHT TRAINING<br>Warm-up<br>5 minutes<br>on the bike. | | |
| **SUPERSET CIRCUIT**<br>**5 sets x 7 reps each**<br>• Bench Press<br>• Hammer Front Pulldowns<br>• Standing Dumbbell Curls | | **SUPERSET CIRCUIT**<br>**3 sets x 8 reps each**<br>• Arnolds<br>• Seated Dumbbell Curls<br>• Tricep Rope Pulldowns | | **SUPERSET CIRCUIT**<br>**3 sets x 8 reps each**<br>• Cybex® Chest Advanced Move<br>• Cybex® Row<br>• Cybex® Reverse Box | | |
| **SUPERSET**<br>**3 sets x 8 reps each**<br>• Wide Grip Front Pulldowns<br>• Dumbbell Incline Press | Spinning, aerobics, or elliptical machine (no longer than 45 minutes)<br>MODERATE INTENSITY | **SUPERSET**<br>**2 sets x 12 reps each**<br>• Rotators<br>• Dumbbell Lateral Raises | Run, hike, or bike<br>45 minutes<br>MODERATE INTENSITY | **SUPERSET**<br>**3 sets x 8 reps each**<br>• "Pec-Dec" Chest Fly<br>• Close Grip Front Pulldowns | Run, hike, or bike<br>45 minutes<br>MODERATE INTENSITY | Walk or bike<br>45 minutes<br>LOW INTENSITY |
| **SUPERSET CIRCUIT**<br>**4 sets x 8 reps each**<br>• Lunges<br>• Smith Machine Squats<br>• Seated Leg Curls | | **SUPERSET**<br>**3 sets x 10 reps**<br>• Cybex® Overhead Press<br>• Cybex® Reverse Fly | | **SUPERSET CIRCUIT**<br>**4 sets x 8 reps each**<br>• Smith Machine Squats<br>• Leg Press<br>• Butt Blaster® | | |
| **SOLO EXERCISE**<br>**4 sets x 15 reps**<br>• Rotary Calf Machine | | **SUPERSET**<br>**3 sets x 10 reps each**<br>• Standing Barbell Curls<br>• Tricep Rope Pulldowns | | **SUPERSET**<br>**3 sets x 10 reps each**<br>• Leg Extensions<br>• Seated Leg Curls | | |
| **SUPERSET**<br>**2 sets x 20 reps each**<br>• Lower Ab Roll Ups<br>• Upper Ab Roll Ups | | **SUPERSET CIRCUIT**<br>**2 sets x 20 reps each**<br>• Lower Ab Roll Ups<br>• Upper Ab Roll Ups<br>• Rotary Torso | | **SUPERSET CIRCUIT**<br>**2 sets x 20 reps each**<br>• Lower Ab Roll Ups<br>• Upper Ab Roll Ups<br>• Rotary Torso | | |
| 20 minutes treadmill | | 20 minutes treadmill | | 20 minutes treadmill | | |
| 2:00 pm<br>POSTWORKOUT MEAL<br>Eat healthy, high protein with carbs. | | 2:00 pm<br>POSTWORKOUT MEAL<br>Eat healthy, high protein with carbs. | | 2:00 pm<br>POSTWORKOUT MEAL<br>Eat healthy, high protein with carbs. | | |

## ADVANCED POWER AND STRENGTH PROGRAM SAMPLE 3x a week
### WEEK FOUR

| MONDAY | TUESDAY | WEDNESDAY | THURSDAY | FRIDAY | SATURDAY | SUNDAY |
|---|---|---|---|---|---|---|
| 11:00 am<br>PREWORKOUT MEAL<br>Eat light, healthy carbs and proteins. | | 11:00 am<br>PREWORKOUT MEAL<br>Eat light, healthy carbs and proteins. | | 11:00 am<br>PREWORKOUT MEAL<br>Eat light, healthy carbs and proteins. | | |
| 12:00 pm<br>WEIGHT TRAINING<br>Warm-up<br>5 minutes<br>on the bike. | | 12:00 pm<br>WEIGHT TRAINING<br>Warm-up<br>5 minutes<br>on the bike. | | 12:00 pm<br>WEIGHT TRAINING<br>Warm-up<br>5 minutes<br>on the bike. | | |
| **SUPERSET CIRCUIT**<br>**5 sets x 7 reps each**<br>• Incline Bench Press<br>• Close Grip Front Pulldowns<br>• Standing Barbell Curls<br><br>**SUPERSET CIRCUIT**<br>**4 sets x 8 reps each**<br>• Lunges<br>• Smith Machine Squats<br>• Seated Leg Curls<br><br>**SUPERSET**<br>**2 sets x 10 reps each**<br>• Hammer Front Pulldowns<br>• Dumbbell Incline Press<br><br>**SOLO EXERCISE**<br>**4 sets x 15 reps**<br>• Rotary Calf Machine<br><br>**SUPERSET**<br>**2 sets x 20 reps each**<br>• Lower Ab Roll Ups<br>• Upper Ab Roll Ups | Spinning, aerobics, or elliptical machine (no longer than 45 minutes)<br>MODERATE INTENSITY | **SUPERSET CIRCUIT**<br>**4 sets x 8 reps each**<br>• Arnolds<br>• Seated Dumbbell Curls<br>• Tricep Rope Pulldowns<br><br>**SUPERSET**<br>**4 sets x 10 reps each**<br>• Cybex® Overhead Press<br>• Cybex® Reverse Fly<br><br>**SUPERSET**<br>**3 sets x 10 reps each**<br>• Standing Hammer Curls<br>• Tricep Rope Pulldowns<br><br>**SUPERSET CIRCUIT**<br>**2 sets x 20 reps each**<br>• Lower Ab Roll Ups<br>• Upper Ab Roll Ups<br>• Rotary Torso | Run, hike, or bike 45 minutes<br>MODERATE INTENSITY | **SUPERSET CIRCUIT**<br>**3 sets x 8 reps each**<br>• Cybex® Chest Advanced Move<br>• Cybex® Row<br>• Cybex® Reverse Box<br><br>**SUPERSET**<br>**3 sets x 8 reps each**<br>• Dumbbell Incline Press<br>• Wide Grip Front Pulldowns<br><br>**SUPERSET CIRCUIT**<br>**4 sets x 10 reps each**<br>• Leg Press<br>• Lunges<br>• Leg Extensions<br>• Seated Leg Curls<br><br>**SUPERSET CIRCUIT**<br>**2 sets x 20 reps each**<br>• Lower Ab Roll Ups<br>• Upper Ab Roll Ups<br>• Rotary Torso | Run, hike, or bike 45 minutes<br>MODERATE INTENSITY | Walk or bike 45 minutes<br>LOW INTENSITY |
| 20 minutes treadmill | | 20 minutes treadmill | | 20 minutes treadmill | | |
| 2:00 pm<br>POSTWORKOUT MEAL<br>Eat healthy, high protein with carbs. | | 2:00 pm<br>POSTWORKOUT MEAL<br>Eat healthy, high protein with carbs. | | 2:00 pm<br>POSTWORKOUT MEAL<br>Eat healthy, high protein with carbs. | | |

## ADVANCED POWER AND STRENGTH PROGRAM SAMPLE 4x a week
### WEEK ONE

| MONDAY | TUESDAY | WEDNESDAY | THURSDAY | FRIDAY | SATURDAY | SUNDAY |
|---|---|---|---|---|---|---|
| 11:00 am<br>PREWORKOUT MEAL<br>Eat light, healthy carbs and proteins. | 11:00 am<br>PREWORKOUT MEAL<br>Eat light, healthy carbs and proteins. | | 11:00 am<br>PREWORKOUT MEAL<br>Eat light, healthy carbs and proteins. | 11:00 am<br>PREWORKOUT MEAL<br>Eat light, healthy carbs and proteins. | | |
| 12:00 pm<br>WEIGHT TRAINING<br>Warm-up<br>5 minutes<br>on the bike. | 12:00 pm<br>WEIGHT TRAINING<br>Warm-up<br>5 minutes<br>on the bike. | | 12:00 pm<br>WEIGHT TRAINING<br>Warm-up<br>5 minutes<br>on the bike. | 12:00 pm<br>WEIGHT TRAINING<br>Warm-up<br>5 minutes<br>on the bike. | | |
| **SUPERSET**<br>2 sets x 15 reps each<br>• Leg Extensions<br>• Prone Leg Curls<br><br>**SUPERSET CIRCUIT**<br>4 sets x 8 reps each<br>• Smith Machine Squats<br>• Seated Leg Curls<br>• Leg Press<br><br>**SOLO EXERCISE**<br>4 sets x 15 reps<br>• Rotary Calf Machine<br><br>**SUPERSET CIRCUIT**<br>2 sets x 20 reps each<br>• Lower Ab Roll Ups<br>• Upper Ab Roll Ups<br>• Rotary Torso<br><br>20 minutes treadmill<br><br>2:00 pm<br>POSTWORKOUT MEAL<br>Eat healthy, high protein with carbs. | **SUPERSET CIRCUIT**<br>4 sets x 8 reps each<br>• Bench Press<br>• Wide Grip Front Pulldowns<br>• Standing Dumbbell Curls<br><br>**SUPERSET**<br>3 sets x 10 reps each<br>• Dumbbell Incline Press<br>• Hammer Front Pulldowns<br><br>**SUPERSET**<br>3 sets x 10 reps each<br>• Cybex® Overhead Press<br>• Cybex® Reverse Fly<br><br>**SUPERSET CIRCUIT**<br>2 sets x 20 reps each<br>• Lower Ab Roll Ups<br>• Upper Ab Roll Ups<br>• Rotary Torso<br><br>20 minutes treadmill<br><br>2:00 pm<br>POSTWORKOUT MEAL<br>Eat healthy, high protein with carbs. | Run, hike, or bike<br>45 minutes<br>MODERATE INTENSITY | **SUPERSET CIRCUIT**<br>3 sets x 10 reps each<br>• Lunges<br>• Leg Extensions<br>• Seated Leg Curls<br><br>**SUPERSET CIRCUIT**<br>3 sets x 15 reps each<br>• Lower Back Hyperextensions<br>• Lower Ab Roll Ups<br>• Upper Ab Roll Ups<br>• Rotary Torso<br><br>**SOLO EXERCISE**<br>3 sets x 15 reps<br>• Rotary Calf Machine<br><br>20 minutes treadmill<br><br>2:00 pm<br>POSTWORKOUT MEAL<br>Eat healthy, high protein with carbs. | **SUPERSET CIRCUIT**<br>4 sets x 10 reps each<br>• Arnolds<br>• Seated Dumbbell Curls<br>• Tricep Rope Pulldowns<br><br>**SUPERSET CIRCUIT**<br>3 sets x 10 reps each<br>• Cybex® Chest Advanced Move<br>• Cybex® Row<br>• Cybex® Reverse Fly<br><br>**SUPERSET**<br>3 sets x 10 reps each<br>• Cybex® Overhead Press<br>• Cybex® Reverse Box<br><br>**SUPERSET**<br>2 sets x 20 reps each<br>• Lower Ab Roll Ups<br>• Upper Ab Roll Ups<br><br>20 minutes treadmill<br><br>2:00 pm<br>POSTWORKOUT MEAL<br>Eat healthy, high protein with carbs. | Run, hike, or bike<br>45 minutes<br>MODERATE INTENSITY | Walk or bike<br>45 minutes<br>LOW INTENSITY |

## ADVANCED POWER AND STRENGTH PROGRAM SAMPLE 4x a week
WEEK TWO

| MONDAY | TUESDAY | WEDNESDAY | THURSDAY | FRIDAY | SATURDAY | SUNDAY |
|---|---|---|---|---|---|---|
| 11:00 am<br>PREWORKOUT MEAL<br>Eat light, healthy carbs and proteins. | 11:00 am<br>PREWORKOUT MEAL<br>Eat light, healthy carbs and proteins. | | 11:00 am<br>PREWORKOUT MEAL<br>Eat light, healthy carbs and proteins. | 11:00 am<br>PREWORKOUT MEAL<br>Eat light, healthy carbs and proteins. | | |
| 12:00 pm<br>WEIGHT TRAINING<br>Warm-up<br>5 minutes<br>on the bike. | 12:00 pm<br>WEIGHT TRAINING<br>Warm-up<br>5 minutes<br>on the bike. | | 12:00 pm<br>WEIGHT TRAINING<br>Warm-up<br>5 minutes<br>on the bike. | 12:00 pm<br>WEIGHT TRAINING<br>Warm-up<br>5 minutes<br>on the bike. | | |
| **SUPERSET**<br>**2 sets x 15 reps each**<br>• Leg Extensions<br>• Seated Leg Curls<br><br>**SUPERSET CIRCUIT**<br>**4 sets x 8 reps each**<br>• Smith Machine Squats<br>• Lunges<br>• Butt Blaster®<br>• Leg Press<br><br>**SOLO EXERCISE**<br>**4 sets x 15 reps**<br>• Rotary Calf Machine<br><br>**SUPERSET CIRCUIT**<br>**2 sets x 20 reps each**<br>• Lower Ab Roll Ups<br>• Upper Ab Roll Ups<br>• Rotary Torso<br><br>20 minutes treadmill<br><br>2:00 pm<br>POSTWORKOUT MEAL<br>Eat healthy, high protein with carbs. | **SUPERSET CIRCUIT**<br>**4 sets x 8 reps each**<br>• Bench Press<br>• Wide Grip Front Pulldowns<br>• Standing Dumbbell Curls<br><br>**SUPERSET CIRCUIT**<br>**3 sets x 10 reps each**<br>• Dumbbell Incline Press<br>• Hammer Front Pulldowns<br>• Cybex® Overhead Press<br>• Cybex® Reverse Fly<br><br>**SUPERSET CIRCUIT**<br>**2 sets x 20 reps each**<br>• Lower Ab Roll Ups<br>• Upper Ab Roll Ups<br>• Rotary Torso<br><br>20 minutes treadmill<br><br>2:00 pm<br>POSTWORKOUT MEAL<br>Eat healthy, high protein with carbs. | Run, hike, or bike<br>45 minutes<br>MODERATE INTENSITY | **SUPERSET CIRCUIT**<br>**3 sets x 10 reps each**<br>• Lunges<br>• Leg Extensions<br>• Seated Leg Curls<br><br>**SUPERSET CIRCUIT**<br>**3 sets x 15 reps each**<br>• Lunges<br>• Lower Ab Roll Ups<br>• Rotary Torso<br>• Lower Back Hyperextensions<br><br>**SOLO EXERCISE**<br>**3 sets x 15 reps**<br>• Rotary Calf Machine<br><br>20 minutes treadmill<br><br>2:00 pm<br>POSTWORKOUT MEAL<br>Eat healthy, high protein with carbs. | **SUPERSET CIRCUIT**<br>**4 sets x 10 reps each**<br>• Arnolds<br>• Seated Dumbbell Curls<br>• Tricep Rope Pulldowns<br><br>**SUPERSET**<br>**4 sets x 8 reps each**<br>• Incline Dumbbell Press<br>• Hammer Front Pulldowns<br><br>**SUPERSET CIRCUIT**<br>**3 sets x 10 reps each**<br>• Cybex® Overhead Press<br>• Cybex® Reverse Fly<br>• Cybex® Reverse Box<br><br>**SUPERSET**<br>**2 sets x 20 reps each**<br>• Lower Ab Roll Ups<br>• Upper Ab Roll Ups<br><br>20 minutes treadmill<br><br>2:00 pm<br>POSTWORKOUT MEAL<br>Eat healthy, high protein with carbs. | Run, hike, or bike<br>45 minutes<br>MODERATE INTENSITY | Walk or bike<br>45 minutes<br>LOW INTENSITY |

## ADVANCED POWER AND STRENGTH PROGRAM SAMPLE 4x a week
### WEEK THREE

| MONDAY | TUESDAY | WEDNESDAY | THURSDAY | FRIDAY | SATURDAY | SUNDAY |
|---|---|---|---|---|---|---|
| 11:00 am<br>PREWORKOUT MEAL<br>Eat light, healthy carbs and proteins. | 11:00 am<br>PREWORKOUT MEAL<br>Eat light, healthy carbs and proteins. | | 11:00 am<br>PREWORKOUT MEAL<br>Eat light, healthy carbs and proteins. | 11:00 am<br>PREWORKOUT MEAL<br>Eat light, healthy carbs and proteins. | | |
| 12:00 pm<br>WEIGHT TRAINING<br>Warm-up<br>5 minutes<br>on the bike. | 12:00 pm<br>WEIGHT TRAINING<br>Warm-up<br>5 minutes<br>on the bike. | | 12:00 pm<br>WEIGHT TRAINING<br>Warm-up<br>5 minutes<br>on the bike. | 12:00 pm<br>WEIGHT TRAINING<br>Warm-up<br>5 minutes<br>on the bike. | | |
| **SUPERSET**<br>**2 sets x 12 reps each**<br>• Leg Extensions<br>• Prone Leg Curls<br><br>**SUPERSET CIRCUIT**<br>**4 sets x 8 reps each**<br>• Smith Machine Squats<br>• Seated Leg Curls<br>• Lunges<br>• Leg Press<br><br>**SOLO EXERCISE**<br>**4 sets x 15 reps**<br>• Rotary Calf Machine<br><br>**SUPERSET CIRCUIT**<br>**2 sets x 20 reps each**<br>• Lower Ab Roll Ups<br>• Upper Ab Roll Ups<br>• Rotary Torso<br><br>20 minutes treadmill<br><br>2:00 pm<br>POSTWORKOUT MEAL<br>Eat healthy, high protein with carbs. | **SUPERSET CIRCUIT**<br>**4 sets x 8 reps each**<br>• Bench Press<br>• Wide Grip Front Pulldowns<br>• Standing Dumbbell Curls<br><br>**SUPERSET CIRCUIT**<br>**3 sets x 10 reps each**<br>• Dumbbell Incline Press<br>• Hammer Front Pulldowns<br>• Cybex® Overhead Press<br>• Cybex® Reverse Fly<br><br>**SUPERSET CIRCUIT**<br>**2 sets x 20 reps each**<br>• Lower Ab Roll Ups<br>• Upper Ab Roll Ups<br>• Rotary Torso<br><br>20 minutes treadmill<br><br>2:00 pm<br>POSTWORKOUT MEAL<br>Eat healthy, high protein with carbs | Run, hike, or bike<br>45 minutes<br>MODERATE INTENSITY | **SUPERSET CIRCUIT**<br>**3 sets x 10 reps each**<br>• Lunges<br>• Leg Extensions<br>• Seated Leg Curls<br><br>**SUPERSET CIRCUIT**<br>**3 sets x 15 reps each**<br>• Lower back Hyperextensions<br>• Lower Ab Roll Ups<br>• Rotary Torso<br><br>**SOLO EXERCISE**<br>**3 sets x 15 reps**<br>• Rotary Calf Machine<br><br>20 minutes treadmill<br><br>2:00 pm<br>POSTWORKOUT MEAL<br>Eat healthy, high protein with carbs. | **SUPERSET CIRCUIT**<br>**4 sets x 10 reps each**<br>• Arnolds<br>• Seated Dumbbell Curls<br>• Tricep Rope Pulldowns<br><br>**SUPERSET CIRCUIT**<br>**3 sets x 10 reps each**<br>• Cybex® Chest Advanced Move<br>• Cybex® Row<br>• Cybex® Reverse Box<br><br>**SUPERSET**<br>**3 sets x 10 reps each**<br>• Cybex® Overhead Press<br>• Cybex® Reverse Box<br><br>**SUPERSET**<br>**2 sets x 20 reps each**<br>• Lower Ab Roll Ups<br>• Upper Ab Roll Ups<br><br>20 minutes treadmill<br><br>2:00 pm<br>POSTWORKOUT MEAL<br>Eat healthy, high protein with carbs. | Run, hike, or bike<br>45 minutes<br>MODERATE INTENSITY | Walk or bike<br>45 minutes<br>LOW INTENSITY |

## ADVANCED POWER AND STRENGTH PROGRAM SAMPLE 4x a week
### WEEK FOUR

| MONDAY | TUESDAY | WEDNESDAY | THURSDAY | FRIDAY | SATURDAY | SUNDAY |
|---|---|---|---|---|---|---|
| 11:00 am<br>PREWORKOUT MEAL<br>Eat light, healthy carbs and proteins. | 11:00 am<br>PREWORKOUT MEAL<br>Eat light, healthy carbs and proteins. | | 11:00 am<br>PREWORKOUT MEAL<br>Eat light, healthy carbs and proteins. | 11:00 am<br>PREWORKOUT MEAL<br>Eat light, healthy carbs and proteins. | | |
| 12:00 pm<br>WEIGHT TRAINING<br>Warm-up<br>5 minutes<br>on the bike. | 12:00 pm<br>WEIGHT TRAINING<br>Warm-up<br>5 minutes<br>on the bike. | | 12:00 pm<br>WEIGHT TRAINING<br>Warm-up<br>5 minutes<br>on the bike. | 12:00 pm<br>WEIGHT TRAINING<br>Warm-up<br>5 minutes<br>on the bike. | | |
| **SUPERSET**<br>**2 sets x 12 reps each**<br>• Leg Extensions<br>• Seated Leg Curls<br><br>**SUPERSET CIRCUIT**<br>**4 sets x 8 reps each**<br>• Smith Machine Squats<br>• Lunges<br>• Butt Blaster®<br>• Leg Press<br><br>**SOLO EXERCISE**<br>**4 sets x 15 reps**<br>• Rotary Calf Machine<br><br>**SUPERSET CIRCUIT**<br>**2 sets x 20 reps each**<br>• Lower Ab Roll Ups<br>• Upper Ab Roll Ups<br>• Rotary Torso<br><br>20 minutes treadmill<br><br>2:00 pm<br>POSTWORKOUT MEAL<br>Eat healthy, high protein with carbs. | **SUPERSET CIRCUIT**<br>**4 sets x 8 reps each**<br>• Incline Bench Press<br>• Wide Grip Front Pulldowns<br>• Standing Dumbbell Curls<br><br>**SUPERSET**<br>**3 sets x 10 reps each**<br>• "Pec-Dec" Chest Fly<br>• Close Grip Front Pulldowns<br><br>**SUPERSET**<br>**3 sets x 10 reps each**<br>• Cybex® Overhead Press<br>• Cybex® Reverse Fly<br><br>**SUPERSET CIRCUIT**<br>**2 sets x 20 reps each**<br>• Lower Ab Roll Ups<br>• Upper Ab Roll Ups<br>• Rotary Torso<br><br>20 minutes treadmill<br><br>2:00 pm<br>POSTWORKOUT MEAL<br>Eat healthy, high protein with carbs. | Run, hike, or bike<br>45 minutes<br>MODERATE INTENSITY | **SUPERSET**<br>**3 sets x 10 reps each**<br>• Leg Extensions<br>• Seated Leg Curls<br><br>**SUPERSET CIRCUIT**<br>**3 sets x 15 reps each**<br>• Lunges<br>• Lower back Hyperextensions<br>• Upper Ab Roll Ups<br>• Lower Ab Roll Ups<br>• Rotary Torso<br><br>**SOLO EXERCISE**<br>**3 sets x 15 reps**<br>• Rotary Calf Machine<br><br>20 minutes treadmill<br><br>2:00 pm<br>POSTWORKOUT MEAL<br>Eat healthy, high protein with carbs. | **SUPERSET CIRCUIT**<br>**4 sets x 10 reps each**<br>• Arnolds<br>• Seated Dumbbell Curls<br>• Tricep Rope Pulldowns<br><br>**SUPERSET**<br>**4 sets x 8 reps each**<br>• Incline Dumbbell Press<br>• Hammer Front Pulldowns<br><br>**SUPERSET CIRCUIT**<br>**3 sets x 10 reps each**<br>• Cybex® Overhead Press<br>• Cybex® Reverse Fly<br>• Cybex® Reverse Box<br><br>**SUPERSET**<br>**2 sets x 20 reps each**<br>• Lower Ab Roll Ups<br>• Upper Ab Roll Ups<br><br>20 minutes treadmill<br><br>2:00 pm<br>POSTWORKOUT MEAL<br>Eat healthy, high protein with carbs. | Run, hike, or bike<br>45 minutes<br>MODERATE INTENSITY | Walk or bike<br>45 minutes<br>LOW INTENSITY |

# glossary

**Abduction**
Movement away from the midline, or center of the body.

**Adduction**
Movement toward the midline, or center of the body.

**ADP (adenosine diphosphate)**
A breakdown by-product of ATP as the result of exercise.

**Aerobic**
An exercise activity that requires oxygen in the fueling of muscle function; generally speaking this is a longer duration exercise.

**Amino acids**
The building blocks of protein utilized in muscle tissue recovery.

**Anaerobic**
An exercise activity of shorter duration (as compared to aerobic exercise) utilizing ATP and CP, and not requiring oxygen at the cellular level.

**Anchoring**
The shoulder blades (scapulae) involves retraction and downward rotation using the rhomboids, middle traps, and lower traps.

**Antagonistic**
Muscles that produce opposite actions across a specific joint; for example, the bicep and tricep muscles that produce flexion and extension, respectively, of the lower arm.

**Antioxidants**
A substance (contained in food or supplements) that helps thwart free radicals and other harmful toxins by reacting with available oxygen.

**ATP (adenosine triphosphate)**
The "fuel" used in muscle function at the cellular level.

**Bilateral**
Involvement of both sides of the body.

**Biomechanical**
The physics (mechanics) of human movement during exercise.

**Carbohydrate**
One of three nutrients used for quick energy. This is the easiest nutrient to be broken down by the body; examples include breads, fruits, and pastas.

**Cardio**
Cardiovascular exercise that involves the heart, lungs, and vascular systems. It is aerobic and commonly an endurance exercise.

**Concentric phase**
The shortening phase of muscle contraction.

**Cool down**
Reducing the intensity of activity toward the end of a workout, facilitating muscular recovery.

**Core posture**
A deep-centered posture that helps stabilize the body during dynamic movements; also utilized in extended durations of static posture.

**Creatine phosphate (CP)**
Combines with ADP to produce ATP, a fuel for fast twitch muscle function.

**Cybex®**
Our preferred brand of exercise equipment, as it is the most biomechanically sound.

**Delts**
The deltoid muscles, anterior, medial, and posterior; the shoulder muscles.

**Eccentric phase**
The lengthening or return phase of muscle contraction, often referred to as the "negative."

**The 8-to-15 Rule**
The parameter of "reps" performed, which helps to determine the proper weight for an exercise.

**Essential fatty acids**
Fats (fatty acids) Omega 3 and 6 fatty acids, that the body requires but cannot produce on its own in adequate supply to meet its physiological needs.

**Extension**
Muscle action that lengthens (moves bones away from each other) or extends a joint.

**External rotation**
Outward rotation at the shoulder or hip joints.

**Fat**
One of three main nutrients that the body requires; necessary for transport and absorption of fat-soluble vitamins.

**Fatty acids**
An intermediate product from the body's processing of fats.

**Flexion**
Muscle action that shortens (moves bones closer to each other) or flexes a joint.

**Foot centers**
Three points on the bottom of the foot on which body weight is distributed.

**Free radicals**
Oxidized by-products that have a negative impact on body function and performance.

**Glutes**
The common name used to refer to the gluteal muscles and buttocks.

**Glycogen**
How the muscles store sugar/glucose; used as part of the fuel source for muscle function.

**Grip**
To grasp, or hold, a bar or handle.

**Hyperextension**
To extend beyond normal range.

**Internal rotation**
Inward rotation at the shoulder or hip joints.

**Iso-lateral**
Single-sided movement.

**Isometric**
Static, nonmoving contraction of a muscle.

**Kinesthetic**
Relating to movement of the human body.

**Knurling mark**
The mark on a weight-lifting bar used to help determine grip position.

**Lactic acid**

A by-product produced by muscle activity.

**Lats**

Common name for the latissimus dorsi muscle, an internal rotator, adductor, and extensor of the shoulder joint.

**Ligament**

Fibrous connective tissue that connects bones to bones.

**Maximum heart rate**

The maximum heart rate that an individual can achieve; varies from individual to individual and between the sexes. Used as a gauge for aerobic exercise intensity.

**Metabolism**

How efficiently the body utilizes fuel (food intake).

**Muscle**

Tissue that can contract and lengthen, producing body motion and function.

**Muscle tone**

The percentage of muscle in a contracted state when the muscle is at rest.

**Overtraining**

A common condition in weight lifters and athletes that involves perpetual muscle tissue breakdown without adequate recovery time.

**Partially hydrogenated oils**

"Bad fats" that are harmful and disruptive to body function; found in processed foods such as peanut butter and potato chips.

**Pec**

Common name for the pectoralis muscles, which form the bulk of the upper chest. The pectoralis major muscle is an internal rotator and adductor of the shoulder joint.

**Posture**

The relative position of the body as it relates to its surroundings and gravity.

**Postworkout meal**

Source of needed protein and carbohydrates to be consumed within 30 to 60 minutes after the workout to facilitate maximum muscle recovery.

**Preworkout meal**

Fuel (food) source for the workout containing carbohydrates and protein to be consumed 30 to 60 minutes prior to the workout. This should *not* be a heavy meal.

**Protein**

One of three main nutrients that the body requires; important for muscle recovery at the cellular level.

**Protraction**

The opposite of *retraction*; forward movement of the scapula.

**Quads**

The common name of the "quadriceps femoris," the anterior thigh muscles (four individual muscles). These four muscles combine to extend the lower leg. One of these muscles also is involved in hip or thigh flexion (rectus femoris).

**Rep**

Repetition; the performance of a given exercise one time. Many "reps" constitute a "set."

**Resistance training**

Training muscles using resistance, typically involving machine or free weights, but can include working against springs (Pilate's reformer).

**Retraction**

Movement of the scapula toward the spine (adduction of the scapula).

**Rotator cuff**

A set of four muscles that stabilize the "gleno-humeral" joint (shoulder) and rotate the upper arm.

**Sacrum**

The bottom of the spine; a fused group of vertebrae shaped like a triangle.

**Saturated fats**

"Bad fats" that are harmful and disruptive to body function; typically solid at room temperature, e.g., butter, lard, and shortening.

**Scapula**

Shoulder blade.

**Sciatic pain**

Hip pain that can "refer," or radiate, down the leg.

**Set**

A specified number of "reps" performed continuously for a given exercise. Typically, the number of "reps" in a "set" is

designed for a specific outcome: strength, power, or endurance.

**Shoulder impingement syndrome**

A condition in which the supraspinatus and biceps tendon are compressed by an unstable shoulder joint, resulting in pain and irritation.

**Skeletal**

The bone structure.

**Stabilization**

The ability to maintain a specific position during movement.

**Sternal-scapular relationship**

The postural relationship, both dynamic and static, between the chest and the shoulder blades.

**Sternum**

The bone in the center of the chest to which the ribs attach.

**Stretching**

Lengthening of the muscle tissue to increase flexibility.

**Superset**

The combination of two or more exercises to be done in sequence. The superset highlighted herein typically involves combining sets of exercises using opposing muscle groups (BAM Superset).

**Supinated**

Palms turned up.

**Supplements**

Additives consumed to supplement nutrition obtained from normal food intake; examples are vitamins, creatine phosphate, and L-carnitine.

**Synergistic muscles**

Muscles working together to produce an efficient common action.

**Tendon**

Fibrous connective tissue that connects muscle to bone.

**Trans-fatty acid**

"Bad fats" that are harmful and disruptive to body function; typically found in hydrogenated foods such as potato chips.

**Warm-up**

An activity performed at low intensity levels to promote blood flow to the muscle tissue.

**Working in**

Sharing or taking turns on the gym equipment. Supersets lend themselves nicely to "working in" with other gym patrons.

**Workout log**

A tool to record and track workouts.

**Workout planner**

A 52-week planning chart for planning workouts; a workout "day timer."

# product information

## EQUIPMENT DISTRIBUTORS

The machines we use in our photos and instructions are primarily Cybex® brand. To obtain the names and locations of health clubs or recreation centers in your area that are equipped with the Cybex® line, contact Cybex® directly.

Cybex International Inc.
10 Trotter Drive
Medway, MA 02053
www.ecybex.com
1-888-go-cybex

Hammer Strength® equipment is a division of Life Fitness.

Life Fitness
5100 North River Road
Schiller Park, IL 60176
1-800-735-3867

The Butt Blaster® machine is produced by Leg Tech, Inc. They appear to be out of business.

## ADDITIONAL RESOURCES

Bob and Jean Anderson's book *Stretching* (ISBN 0-936070-22-6), published by Shelter Publications, can be ordered by calling 1-800-333-1307 or by visiting www.stretching.com.

The Better Posture product line includes posture improvement videos and DVDs, as well as a CD-ROM covering ergonomics. These products were produced by author Dale Greenwald, CSCS. For further information or to order call 1-303-494-4931 or visit www.betterposture .com.

## SPECIALTY PRODUCTS

Polar Heart Rate monitors can be ordered by calling 1-800-227-1314 or by visiting www.polarusa.com.

Swiss Balls can be obtained through many distributors; however, a dependable site that stands behind their products and gives quality customer service is www.simplefitnesssolutions.com. They can also be reached at 1-866-283-4242.

### Weekly Workout Planner

**WE HAVE CREATED A WEEKLY WORKOUT PLANNER TO ACCOMPANY THIS BOOK. THIS IS A 52-WEEK WORKOUT "DAY TIMER" THAT WILL HELP YOU TO CHART AND CREATE YOUR WORKOUTS. IT IS AVAILABLE AS A CD-ROM OR AS A BOOK (ISBN 0-9755141-1-3), AND BOTH CAN BE PURCHASED AT WWW.WORKOUTBOOK.COM OR AT SELECT BOOKSTORES AND GYMS.**

# index

# Index

# Index

# about the authors

Dale Greenwald, CSCS, is a nationally recognized lecturer and exercise physiologist. Mr. Greenwald competed for 7 years in the sport of powerlifting, recording 3 state championships, 4 state records, 2 national records, and achieving the status of a 4-time All-American. However, after sustaining a career-ending injury, Mr. Greenwald changed the focus of his training from competition to learning how to lift with injuries. After graduating from the University of Colorado with a degree in Exercise Physiology in 1989, Mr. Greenwald began his work in the field of exercise wellness and rehabilitation. The majority of Mr. Greenwald's clients either have sustained an injury or have had little or no experience using weights or lifting machines. His practice continues to focus on helping to educate and instruct individuals on correct lifting and exercise technique. Mr. Greenwald's other contributions to the field include several patented shoulder rehabilitation devices, his work as editor of "The Ergonomics Review" email newsletter, and the production of a postural video and ergonomic CD-ROM. Now, Mr. Greenwald proudly brings his BAM Superset™ system and specialized exercise technique to the wellness community.

Dale lives in Boulder, Colorado, with his wife, Linda, and two boys, Bryce and Matt.

Erik Miller is a certified personal trainer with a strong background in human anatomy. Mr. Miller maintains his own private personal training practice working primarily with individuals from the professional world who want to pursue an active lifestyle and remain competitive and injury-free. Mr. Miller has successfully integrated the BAM Superset™ system into this practice. He also uses the BAM Superset™ system in training individuals who have not had success with their own exercise programs, enabling them to fulfill their fitness goals.

Erik lives in Boulder, Colorado, with his wife and two daughters. He is an avid outdoorsman, enjoying skiing, and hiking in the Rocky Mountain West.